Building Tolerance to Life's Inevitabilities

By

Trent L. Culver

Author's Note

The information presented in this book is not a substitute for seeking professional care tailored to your specific situation. Each person and family has unique needs that require proper therapy and medical advice. This book is intended solely for educational purposes and should not be considered the definitive treatment for your individual needs. If you find yourself needing immediate professional care, please contact your local emergency number or mental health crisis hotline for immediate assistance.

It is important to understand that this publication aims to provide accurate and authoritative information on the subject matter covered. However, the author is not engaged in providing psychological, legal, or any other professional services. If you require expert assistance or counseling, it is advisable to seek the services of a competent professional.

With these in mind, I invite you to explore the content

of this book, which aims to offer valuable insights and guidance. May it empower you to uncover your true potential and enable you to lead a more connected and fulfilling life.

Dedication

To my late parents: Thank you and thank you. To my brother, thank you for your unwavering loyalty. To my beautiful wife, thank you for your unconditional love. To Chiquita and Mookie, thank you for your timely emotional love.

To all who want to take the POWER BACK!

Acknowledgment

I would like to thank the following psychological disciplines that changed my life:

First and foremost, I am grateful to Adlerian Psychology for the invaluable lessons I learned during my time at Adler University. The emphasis on genuine empathy and the transformative power of encouragement deeply resonated with me. The seeds planted during those formative years continue to influence my approach to building meaningful connections and creating a supportive environment for others.

The introduction of Cognitive Behavioral Therapy (CBT) marked a pivotal moment in my journey. The understanding of how our thoughts and interpretations shape our emotions and behaviors was a revelation. CBT provided me with the tools to challenge negative thinking patterns, reframe perspectives, and cultivate greater emotional well-being. It was a transformative experience that forever changed my relationship with my own mind.

And lastly, in recent years, the discovery of Positive Psychology has been a beacon of light. It has shown me that amidst the challenges of life, we possess an abundance of inherent strengths and resilience. Positive Psychology has shifted my focus towards nurturing these strengths, fostering optimism, and promoting personal growth. Its profound impact has allowed me to embrace the inherent goodness within myself and others, instilling a sense of hope and possibility.

I would like to extend my deepest gratitude to the founders, professors, practitioners, and researchers in Adlerian Psychology, Cognitive Behavioral Therapy, and Positive Psychology. Your contributions have not only enriched my life but also inspired my dedication to helping others unlock their potential and live fulfilling lives.

About the Author

Dr. Culver is a licensed clinical psychologist and certified alcohol and drug counselor who is deeply committed to providing a holistic approach to mental health. With a career spanning over two decades, his unwavering mission has been to help individuals and families unlock their true potential and lead lives that are deeply connected and fulfilling.

As a public speaker, coach, and author, Dr. Culver is dedicated to offering genuine and meaningful guidance that propels individuals further in life. He understands the power of authentic work that resonates with individuals, allowing them to make thoughtful transformations.

In addition to his professional pursuits, Dr. Culver

is passionate about the beautiful outdoors, sports, music, and movies and integrates these interests into his work, employing different methods to provide a deeper understanding of oneself, personal goals, and values.

Table of Contents

Foreword

In the pages that follow, Dr. Trent L. Culver aims to embark you on a transformative journey guided by his wisdom and expertise. As a psychologist, he embraces a fundamental role - one that is rooted in trust, empathy, and a nonjudgmental stance. The foundation of the therapeutic relationship, which he forged early in his career while running a teen center, is built upon trust, effective listening, respect, and genuine care.

Moving forward, you will find a tapestry of knowledge presented in various styles: from written words to captivating parables, thought-provoking metaphors, and even vibrant visuals. He understands that each person has their own unique way of absorbing information, and so he considered it essential to cater to different learning preferences. Whether you are a visual learner who finds inspiration in images or someone who thrives on metaphors and narratives, Dr. Culver wanted to ensure that this book speaks to you just as it should.

To further enhance accessibility, an audio version of this book is also available. He recognizes that auditory learners often find great resonance in spoken words and wants to provide an immersive experience that caters to their needs. It is his belief that knowledge should transcend limitations and be accessible to everyone, regardless of their learning style.

Dr. Culver respects the complexity of the human journey and understands that each individual's path is unique. Rather than making lofty claims, his intention is to provide you with valuable insights, practical tools, and diverse perspectives that can empower you on your personal quest.

Whether you choose to read this book in its written form or immerse yourself in the accompanying audio version, know that Dr. Culver has poured his heart and soul into crafting a comprehensive and engaging resource.

It is my pleasure to introduce you to the remarkable insights and guidance contained within these pages. As you immerse yourself in this book, I encourage you to reflect on your own journey, embracing the challenges and cultivating your unique strengths.

- Trent L. Culver

Page Blank Intentionally

Chapter 1: Tolerance

"Within the embrace of tolerance lies the seed of serenity, while the rejection of differences sows' seeds of discord and unrest."

The word tolerance is from the early fifteenth century, from the Latin word 'tolerantia.' This word was originally intended to endure distress or offer support. In 1765, it was associated with a more modern definition; it began to denote a tendency to free oneself from judgment.

Personally, I view tolerance as enduring distress by leaning into the cause without judgment, not from others and definitely not ourselves. Tolerance helps to encourage individualism and the expression of personal interests and beliefs. There are many other words that can be used in place of tolerance.

Some synonyms for tolerance can be concession, acceptance, impartiality, parity, fairness, equivalence, etc. Tolerance is not passive. Rather, it is an active approach based on mutual understanding and respect from within ourselves, especially where there are differences of opinion, which is what it requires. Tolerance is the most robust basis for peace and reconciliation within ourselves. Tolerance is necessary for all aspects of life, at all levels and phases, because it plays a crucial role in establishing a healthy mindset. But tolerance is not easy because we rely so heavily on our own experiences and worldview lens, which at times can be subjective and even biased.

Building tolerance can be challenging because we are confronted with the uneasiness of a possible inevitability. For example, trying out for a sport, studying for an exam, inviting someone over, going to a job interview, working on a project, going out with friends, engaging in a romantic relationship, etc. In order to achieve the above things, we must expose ourselves to potential fears, rejections, failures, and changes, which can create overwhelming feelings that turn off our switch to build tolerance. It is these emotions that cause us to retreat to a more comfortable environment that perpetuates the uncomfortable feelings in the long run. As we lean in, we build a tolerance to feeling vulnerable, and it gradually becomes less painful the next time.

True tolerance calls for disagreement, not approval, and that too, from ourselves, not others, or society. The foundation phrase for tolerance means to bear or endure. It'd lose meaning altogether if we attempt to force "tolerance" to intend settlement and approval. Tolerance must not be mistaken as an expression of apathy or laissez-faire.

Without engagement with alterity, tolerance loses its essential meaning as a framework for integrating difference and becomes irrelevant in its productive function.

Cultivating a spirit of tolerance can bring healing and meaning in life in unimaginable ways. Think of your life as a journey to the top of a mountain. If the base of the mountain symbolizes the day you were born, and the top symbolizes your last day on Earth, imagine where you are on that mountain today at your current age. Imagine walking slowly and steadily up that mountain to this day. Imagine stopping along the way, turning around, and looking back down the path you've traveled since birth. Reflect on your path so far with compassionate curiosity.

What obstacles, difficulties, and challenges have you overcome to get to where you are now? What lessons have you learned? Who did you help along the way? How did you help them? Who has helped you? How have you actually grown as a person? What do you know about yourself now that you didn't before on your journey? Now, what can be done differently in the future with the knowledge you have acquired?

Developing tolerance means you are more prone to endure the stress, fear, and sadness that come with adversity and find a way to bounce back from setbacks. Everyone experiences a variety of stresses in the course of their lives.

These stresses can range from everyday annoyances to important events such as losing a job, divorce, or the death of a loved one. Whether the stress is big or small, your ability to tolerate stress can play a role in how you handle the situation. We all go through bad times, experience loss, disappointment, and change, and we all feel sad, anxious, and stressed at different times in our lives. But building tolerance may help you face uncertainty with less fear and get through even the darkest days. If you are more sensitive to emotional stress and find it difficult to cope with difficulties or adversity, it is important not to view this as some sort of character flaw. Tolerance is not a macho trait and is not fixed. It is a continuous process that needs effort to build and maintain over time.

Hard times don't last forever, but by their very nature, they rarely end quickly. As we look for a way through the darkness, we must find ways and things that keep us motivated to move forward. How does one deal with and build tolerance against these feelings of stress, depression, disappointment, anger, frustration, uncertainty, and anxiety?

A King once asked one of his men to write for him something that would turn his sadness feeling into happiness and his happiness into sadness. The soldier just smiled, scribbled something on a piece of paper, and handed it to the

King. The King opened the folded note, and his eyes widened.

The note read, "THIS TIME SHALL PASS TOO."

So, thinking of it in a positive light, bad times pass too. While it's often difficult to imagine something good from challenging experiences, building tolerance can help you find positivity in the difficulties you've faced.

Words like these are motivation to endure challenging times in your life. Hang on to such words because, in the end, no period of life is meant to last forever. Celebrate small victories as you navigate life's stormy seas; take a moment to savor your conquests. Taking note and digesting these small victories can give you a welcomed break from all the stress and negativity you face and encourage you to keep going.

For example, if you're looking for a job, an interview isn't as important as the job, but it is a sign of progress, a step in the right direction. There is always something you won't be able to control in the situation. By putting your focus and energy on what you can control, you may no longer have time to worry about the uncertain and unpleasant aspects of the situation. This focus shift is more productive than spending time worrying about things you can't control.

Individuals who are tolerant are able to effectively bypass the established process for completing tasks. They don't mind breaking the rules when necessary, and they don't mind others doing the same. For them, the rules serve business, not the other way around. They forgive when someone else makes a mistake, even repeatedly. Tolerance encourages forgiveness within ourselves and others because we appreciate and understand the struggles when facing uncertainty. We respect ourselves and others who confront inevitabilities almost as if it were an unwritten law to follow.

As you work to develop more tolerance in your own life, you can feel happier knowing that you can forge your way through challenging times. It's hard to be bitter about what you don't have when you focus your energy on what you have. The key to internal happiness is to realize that you already do have everything you need to be happy. When you understand that happiness and acceptance are inside jobs, you become less likely to demand them from other people and situations. You are the only one with the combination to this internal safe - as it should be! However, difficult situations, experiences, and critics are going to try and take them from you, but with the right mindset, you can protect them.

So, the next time life throws you a curveball,

remember that you have the power to choose how you react. Don't give away the treasures of your internal safe to anyone or anything that doesn't deserve them. Instead, hold on to them tightly, knowing that they're yours and no one can take them away from you. In the end, your happiness and sense of acceptance are not dependent on anyone else but you, so cherish them and keep them safe!

Always remember that if you are able to give yourself unconditional love, then you will be able to give unconditional love to others. Being tolerant and forgiving can create inner peace like no other. Tolerance is your ability to deal with discomfort. It's your ability to resist the 'yuck' in your life and go after what you want. Tolerance can be thought of as mental and emotional endurance. Cultivating tolerance can be life-changing. Tolerance bestows grace, offers understanding, and enables a deeper relationship with oneself.

Inevitabilities That Present in Life

Inevitabilities refer to events or outcomes that are certain to happen, regardless of any efforts to prevent or alter them. They are the unavoidable consequences of a particular situation or set of circumstances, and they are often seen as natural or predetermined outcomes that cannot be avoided or changed. Inevitabilities can manifest in various forms, such as physical laws, social trends, or personal destinies, and they can be both positive and negative. While they may seem daunting or even frightening at times, inevitabilities can also provide a sense of stability and predictability in an otherwise unpredictable world.

Inevitabilities are like the unrelenting tides of the ocean, constantly ebbing and flowing with an irresistible force that no human effort can ever fully control or contain. They remind us that no matter how much we may strive to alter the course of our lives, there are some things that are simply beyond our power to change. Inevitabilities are the great equalizers of the world, showing us that no matter who we are or what we may do, we are all subject to the same inexorable march of time and the unyielding force of destiny. And yet, in their very inevitability, there is also a strange comfort to be found, for they remind us that no matter what trials we may face or what challenges may lie ahead, there are some things that will always remain constant and unchanging, giving us the strength to face whatever the future may bring with courage and resilience.

When we are unsure or uncertain about the outcomes of inevitabilities, we can often resort to a way of thinking that is negative. Inevitabilities can create universal emotions like guilt, shame, depression, sadness, anger, frustration, and fear. When facing inevitabilities, we can be prone to self-sabotaging behavior and become drawn to patterns and choices that subvert and erode our relationship with ourselves, others, and the world. Inevitabilities are like the weather - we may not be able to control them, but we can certainly learn to dress for them and make the most of whatever comes our way. And this is where the idea behind this book comes in - a bit of like a guide to weathering life's storms on how to develop the tolerance and flexibility we need to thrive, no matter what life throws our way.

There are no generation gaps when confronted with inevitabilities—they are experienced at any age.

Change is the only constant in life. From small changes to big life changes, changes happen around us every day. Shifting schools or jobs due to various reasons, one has to face the change in atmosphere, has to make new friends/colleagues; basically, start from scratch, yet again. But in order to succeed, this change is inevitable.

Every chapter of life inevitably comes to an end. As said, *"Nothing lasts forever."* Now, be it a relationship, success, happiness, bad time, or any other aspect of life. Either way, the end is inevitable.

Another thing that is inevitable is disagreements and conflicts. At a point in life, you will have disagreements, and these can even lead to conflicts. Disagreement and conflicts are, without a doubt, unavoidable, as everyone has their own way of thinking, but should they be a stone in the path?

Perfectionism is another factor that can prevent you from progressing. Failure is inevitable and omnipresent. It is the one thing that we all have in common. But expecting perfection can be crippling because there is no such thing. I remember a teacher saying, "Why do you think they invented an erasure?" Because we all make mistakes. For example, failure can take many forms: failing to close a deal, not getting the academic grades you hoped for, a breakup in a relationship, or any type of general setback. The problem with our inability to deal with failure is that it leads to success, which is harder to come by.

The other inevitable aspect of life is that no matter how accurately you anticipate, eventually, everyone will surprise you. People, just like us, are going through their own ordeals in life, things outsiders can never anticipate or know about.

But you do see their reactions, the disagreements, the conflicts. Oftentimes, even you can be on the receiving end.

So, you just assume that you are drifting away from them or that they don't understand you. What you have no idea about is what they are internally or even externally facing.

Moving on, let's talk about fear. Fear is one strong emotion. It arises with the threat of harm, whether physical, emotional, or psychological, real or imagined, and as a result, it is inevitable. Fear creates a hyper-alertness that can overwhelm us and produces startled responses based on chaos through our flight or fight instincts. It is also one of the biggest obstacles that keep many of us from achieving our goals.

Another inevitability can be missed opportunities. Certainly, at one point or another, we all miss an opportunity for one reason or another. It can be a missed important interview or even a missed opportunity to attend a party or sporting event. But missing out is inevitable.

Time waits for no one. It flies and passes faster than one can realize. Aging and getting old is tough and inevitable to come to terms with. You think you have a whole life ahead of you to make amends, but suddenly, you are just left reminiscing if you did get out in front of this brevity.

Alongside aging, death is inevitable. Death marks that moment when your physical body stops working to survive. You breathe your last breath. Your heart stops beating. Your brain stops. Other vital organs, including the kidneys and liver, stop. All of the systems in your body that are powered by these organs also shut down, rendering them unable to carry out the continuous processes understood by simple living.

Although grief is an inevitable part of life, the loss of a loved one is often unexpected and difficult to cope with, even when the loss is expected. It stirs myriad complex emotions, and its reality dwarfs anything you've heard about grief. There is no way to prepare for grief. Grief is a natural response to any kind of loss, especially the death of someone. It goes beyond mere sadness and often evokes feelings of confusion, doubt, guilt, anger, and other complex emotions. There is no one right way to grieve this inevitable - everyone responds to loss and grief differently.

The Pullback - Homeostasis

Imagine going from not working out physically to getting after it at the gym. We would naturally want to go back to sitting and keep all the calories rather than losing them. At first, you resist - it feels uncomfortable and unfamiliar.

But over time, you begin to adapt and get stronger in

new ways. This is a bit like how homeostasis can inhibit our ability to build a tolerance to life's challenges. When we're in a state of homeostasis, we tend to stick with what's comfortable and familiar and avoid anything that feels challenging or outside of our comfort zone. This can make it difficult for us to build up our resilience and tolerance to stress and adversity.

For example, imagine you've been working at the same job for years, and you're comfortable with the routine and the people you work with. But then, your boss announces that the company is restructuring, and you'll need to learn new skills and work with new colleagues. At first, this can feel unsettling and uncomfortable - you may feel like you're losing control over your work life. But if you can push past that initial discomfort and embrace the challenge, you may find that you're capable of more than you thought.

Homeostasis is not just a concept that applies to our bodies and minds - it can also be applied to organizations, individuals, and families. When faced with the prospect of change or reorganization, it's natural to feel resistance or hesitation. We are creatures of habit, and our natural impulse is to maintain the status quo. In organizations, homeostasis can manifest in a number of ways. For example, a company may resist adopting new technologies or processes, even if they could improve efficiency or profitability. This can be due to a variety of factors, including a fear of the unknown, a cultural reluctance to deviate from established procedures, or a lack of awareness about the benefits of change. However, if an organization can push past this initial resistance and embrace new ideas, it may be able to thrive in a rapidly changing market.

Now, the question is: Can inevitabilities be seen as a threat? Can inevitabilities instinctively override the adjustment and return us back to the dysfunctional homeostatic level, such as the fear of success or failure? Fear of change? Fear of conflict or disagreement? Fear of time? Fear of missed opportunities? Fear of getting older? Fear of death? Fear of loss? Indeed. We, as humans, often perceive a lot of inevitabilities as threats. Inevitabilities are events or circumstances that are bound to happen, regardless of our actions or intentions. They can range from trivial things like the change of seasons to major life events like the aging process or the inevitability of death.

While some inevitabilities can be seen as positive or neutral, others can be perceived as a threat. For example, the inevitability of death is something that many people fear. Similarly, the inevitability of getting older can also be a source of anxiety for some people. The fear of aging is often tied to the fear of losing one's youth, vitality, and independence.

When faced with these types of inevitabilities, it is common for people to feel a sense of helplessness or powerlessness. This feeling can lead to a desire to return to a dysfunctional homeostatic level where things feel more familiar and comfortable. This instinctual response can be dangerous because it can prevent us from making necessary changes in our lives and adapting to new circumstances.

The concept of feeling inevitabilities as a threat can halt our growth forward because it can lead to a mindset that is focused on avoidance and self-protection rather than growth and progress. When faced with an inevitable outcome, such as the possibility of failure, it is natural for some individuals to feel a sense of helplessness and defeat. This feeling can lead to self-sabotaging behaviors such as procrastination or avoidance of the task at hand.

Have you ever been on the cusp of achieving a major goal or milestone in your life, only to suddenly find yourself taking two steps back instead of one step forward? This experience can be frustrating and confusing, especially when you feel like you've worked so hard to get where you are. But why does it happen?

One reason for this phenomenon is that our brains are wired to maintain a state of equilibrium or homeostasis. We develop habits and routines that help us feel comfortable and safe, even if those habits and routines are not necessarily in our best interest. These patterns of behavior become deeply ingrained in our neural pathways, making it difficult to break free from them.

When we are on the brink of achieving a goal, we are often pushing ourselves outside of our comfort zones and challenging these established patterns of behavior. This can be scary and uncomfortable, triggering a stress response in our brains that sends us back to our old ways of behaving. Our brain tells us that it's safer to retreat to what we know rather than continue to push forward into the unknown. To overcome this tendency to relapse into old patterns of behavior, it's important to be mindful of our thoughts and actions. Recognizing the signs of relapse, such as negative self-talk or avoidance behaviors, can help us catch ourselves before we fall back into old habits. We can also rewire our brains by consciously choosing new behaviors and practicing them consistently over time. This takes effort and commitment, but it's a way to break free from old patterns and achieve lasting change. Remember, change is possible, even when it feels difficult or uncomfortable.

Inevitabilities can create emotional states characterized by pain, numbness, sadness, withdrawal, embarrassment, disconnection, anger, fear, anxiety, or even shame. These raw emotions may cause severe emotional pain. However, the way we think about inevitabilities is our choice, which may or may not lead to suffering. This book is about waking up to guided self-discovery and taking back the life you deserve, even in the face of inevitabilities. As you continue to hike your life mountain, you may even find the concepts and research discussed in this book to be useful in terms of your self-exploration on the mountain top.

As you turn the page to the next chapter, let's take a moment to pause and reflect on what we just talked about – falling back into old habits. It's a frustrating experience that can leave you feeling defeated and helpless. But what if I told you that there's a way to break free from this cycle?

By taking a few minutes to explore when and why you sabotage yourself and relapse into homeostasis, you can gain valuable insight into your own thought patterns and behaviors. What triggers this cycle for you? When are you at your most vulnerable? What thoughts are going through your head when you start to slip back into old habits?

Identifying these patterns can be the key to unlocking

lasting change. By recognizing the thoughts and beliefs that are holding you back, you can begin to challenge and change them. It's not an easy process, but it's one that's worth the effort. So, before you move on to the next chapter, take a few minutes to explore your own patterns of behavior. You might be surprised at what you discover.

Chapter 2: Our Struggles Strengthen Us

"Embrace your deepest fears, for within them lies the path to healing. Open the closed doors of your heart, softening the hardened barriers that obstruct your growth. Trust in the rhythm of life's journey, for it holds the key to your ultimate healing."

The struggle in life is something that everyone deals with. Whether its relationship conflicts, financial or work-related issues, academics, or sports, we can feel like everything is piling up on us. It can feel like the world is pinned against us, and it's not playing a role. You try, but it gets harder and harder. I understand these feelings very well.

In our society, we often view struggle as something negative, something to be avoided at all costs. We associate it with failure, weakness, and shame. But the truth is that struggle is an inherent part of the human experience, and it's something that we all must face at one point or another. It's about facing challenges head-on, even when it's difficult or uncomfortable. Without struggle, there can be no growth or progress. Sometimes we need to get lost to find our authentic selves. Unfortunately, our cultural stigma surrounding struggle has led us to draw the wrong conclusions. We look for success stories and try to emulate them without taking into account the struggles and challenges those individuals faced along the way. Society often focuses on the end result rather than the process of struggle and growth that leads to that result. This has created a skewed and unrealistic viewpoint. But the art of struggle is just as important, if not more so, than the end result. It's time for us to reframe our understanding of struggle and embrace the challenges that come our way as opportunities for growth and development.

I believe how we lead or move forward or backward is the sum of our thoughts and beliefs about this life journey. Many people don't realize how much their thinking affects their quality of life. I'm not saying life is always easy because life itself is definitely a challenge. When we fight against the natural rhythms of life, we create resistance, and that resistance leads to struggle. In battle, there is no joy and seldom any reward.

The reality is that problems won't disappear on their own. It's only by facing them head-on and making a sincere effort to find solutions that we can overcome them. I define truth as those pieces of reality that no longer scare us. As we move on in life, we may encounter many obstacles and problems that can distract us from our true path causing us sadness, pain, and heartache. We've all been there...

You stick to your diet for a week and then break it off with a weekend binge.

You commit to exercising more, hit the gym for two days, and then struggle to get off the couch after a hectic day at work.

You set a vision for your career and embrace the possibilities, only to get carried away by the day-to-day responsibilities and take months to return to your dream. Academically, you do well on the first exam of the semester, only to bomb the next exam because of procrastination and not putting in the effort needed to excel.

A team performs well in the first half of the match, but unfortunately, due to overconfidence in the not-yet-win, they do not put in enough effort in the second half and lose the almost-won match.

An anxious teenager feels empowered by not having panic attacks for a few weeks, only to backslide and have it come back the following week.

A husband controls his anger issues and works on improving his relationship with his wife for weeks, only to slip up, give in to his anger, and ruin it all after having a bad day.

An alcoholic mother works on herself and fights her urges for the sake of her children, only to slip up and give in as she feels overwhelmed.

A thriving business can close, and its success can come to an end due to various reasons. So, we try to hold on to the present and resist going forward.

But these setbacks don't make you a failure. They just make you human. Even the most successful individuals in the world make mistakes in their habits. What sets them apart isn't their willpower or motivation but their ability to quickly get back on track, which defines the 'bounce back.' You don't need superhuman willpower. You just need strategies to help you get back on the rewrite. Experiencing failure or finding something difficult allows us to progress in learning. The growth process is a process of 'falling and getting up.'

Losing is really winning. We learn a lot from defeats! We learn from failures, mistakes, adversities, and setbacks. The way we win is by going ahead with thoughts that promote a positive blueprint, laying our foundation for our next victory over previous losses. Success begins with these values. Nobody wins every time. No one. Steve Jobs was actually fired from the company he started!

When he returned to Apple more than ten years later, he made it the most profitable company in the world. Michael Jordan suffered devastating losses for six seasons.

He did not win the championship until his seventh season in the NBA. J.K. Rowling endured depression, physical and emotional abuse, poverty, and humiliation. Now we know her as one of the most successful authors of all time.

Just as anyone can win, anyone can lose too. Through our experiences, we evolve and discover our own definitions of success. Growth doesn't happen just because something is bound to occur. It's the process of grappling with challenges that lead to growth. You have to be willing to engage even if you think it probably won't work. Probably usually denotes that the odds are not in your favor. But make no mistake: probably doesn't equal possible.

The world has been blessed with many contributions from great women and men who aspired to do something special that was highly unlikely at the time. Losing leads to winning, and winning leads to success. It is imperative that you define success for yourself in your schooling, career, hobby, or business venture by defining what success means to you. Set measurable goals that support your definition of success. You are the architect of your own plan, whether it is a short-term plan or a long-term plan. Because once you commit to it both mentally and emotionally, you'll be better able to invest and immerse your mind to succeed in what it is you choose to do. Success is deserved.

Struggling through difficult situations can help you stay humble and rooted, especially if you approach those struggles as opportunities for learning and growth. Leaders know that through the losses, we begin to build the next win. We are forced to go back to the drawing board and create plans that will propel us to the life of our dreams. Losing is not actually losing because we learn something from it despite the intense emotional pain it may cause at the moment. Losses are important and inevitable.

Comfort - what a beautiful word to describe such a wonderful state of mind. It is human nature's universal trait that we seek comfort. You would assume that comfort can be a goal worth pursuing, but it is actually one of humanity's greatest built-in impediments to growth. If we weren't connected to our affinity for comfort, our chances for a better livable life and world would be unfathomable. It may be that looking for too much comfort keeps us from our goals and stunts the personal growth necessary to achieve them.

When we feel good, life feels comfortable and easy. The aura of comfort is a place where we can regenerate after a hard day's work. Comfort compels us to stay and revel in the lack of stress that accompanies this loved state. But do we get stronger mentally or psychically? I doubt it. Growth can create a feeling of uncomfortableness due to fear. We need to embrace fear head-on in order for growth to happen, and then true learning occurs, which is the idea that we can be comfortable while feeling uncomfortable. Growing up is supposed to be uncomfortable.

Being new to something can be uncomfortable and embarrassing. And these are hard feelings to endure. But they are the inevitable growing pains that come with learning, developing, and improving at anything. Know that being a beginner takes courage.

Understand that it takes vulnerability and courage to face weaknesses and try new things. While learning is primarily intellectual, methodological, and behavioral in nature, the experience of learning is primarily emotional. Mostly, it's the emotional experience of learning to be a beginner and making mistakes, often publicly, that often keeps people from learning. Being a beginner, clumsy, uncoordinated, and inept can feel embarrassing. But it's not. It is just a phase we must go through to become graceful, coordinated, and competent. And our unwillingness to experience this phase can hinder our future growth. This is especially true in areas where you are already an expert.

Feel everything. That's what I call emotional courage. If you are ready to feel anything: embarrassment, failure, discomfort, and then you can do anything. You've accepted the truth—those pieces of reality that no longer scare us. And whatever you do, don't stop learning. Make an effort, especially in areas where you've already had success, so you can continue to improve. Keep thinking of yourself as a learner. Take risks to try new things.

Is there a choice of what makes you feel comfortable or uncomfortable? How influential is your aura of comfort in your daily activities? What must life be like if you didn't have boundaries preventing you from going beyond your previously established comfort limits? Our aura of comfort may have more impact on our behavior than anyone can imagine.

Comfort is experienced through the presence of many perceived factors, such as rest, homeostasis, lack of stress, and control. Feelings, good or bad, are caused by the release of chemicals that are stimulated by our thoughts or our environment. When you're comfortable and life behaves the way you prefer, your brain can release chemicals like dopamine and serotonin that create feelings and sensations that come across as good.

When you are unfamiliar or uncomfortable with a situation, you may experience negative feelings such as fear, anxiety, or stress. These feelings are the opposite of comfort and are caused by the release of chemicals from your brain, like adrenaline and glutamate. Our bodies release these chemicals in preparation for dealing with potentially harmful or undesirable situations. They make our negative feelings; our hearts beat faster, and our bodies sweat. The severity of this release of chemicals depends on how far we are from our aura of comfort. Our aura of comfort acts as an inner governor that has a mind of its own. It doesn't want us to do anything outside of your preset limits.

We can all understand that some of our boundaries are there to protect us from harm and are necessary for our survival. But oftentimes, we forget this aspect of life and become impatient. You can consider the example of a man here who sowed a seed in the ground. He waited a day, then two days, then three. But finally, when the days became a week, and he saw no results, he couldn't wait any longer and dug up the seed. There, he witnessed small, almost unnoticeable roots working their way to penetrate the soil.

He tampered with the roots and placed the soil back, trying to help the now-growing plant, but instead, he ruined it. A week turned to weeks, and he saw no activity. The seed didn't even outgrow the soil as it had been ruined now. In the next few days, concerned, he tried to shelter it from rain and any harshness nature threw at it. What he didn't realize was that nature was doing its job perfectly, and he didn't need to interfere. The seed had to go through all the harsh weather, all the hot and cold, to become an ever-standing, strong tree.

We cannot do other's jobs, especially nature's, as it prepares us. Sometimes fighting is just what we need in our lives. If we were allowed to go through life unhindered, it would paralyze us. We wouldn't be as strong as we could have been, and we could never soar. Life without any obstacle would do nothing except cripple us. There are many limits when we approach or cross these obstacles, and they prevent us from doing the things we must not do to achieve the desired future.

Fear is one main creator of our boundaries. Fears are interpreted in unique ways by all of us and help create part of our identity. We have a strong tendency to avoid the things that provoke our fears and seek out the things in life that comfort us. Unfortunately, sometimes, what brings us comfort can be the polar opposite of achieving our goals and what we really want in this life.

Changes are often outside of our aura of comfort because they are new territory for us. As we know, everything in life is constantly changing. The more we entrench ourselves in our aura of comfort, the more difficult a change event can become. Overcoming our fears and processing the emotions triggered by the chemicals created in our bodies is an act of effort that can only be done with the intention to do so. We are all capable of overcoming this process.

Growing is about stepping outside your aura of comfort and embracing the feelings associated with being vulnerable and uncomfortable. Once this is achieved, your potential can be limitless.

Now let's talk about how we physically need to struggle to manifest our greatness. Manifesting is turning your dreams into reality; it requires you to take proactive steps to achieve what you desire.

You shouldn't expect it to happen right away, but while it's a long process, it is kind of a very small price to pay for a profound impact on your life. We all experience the time when we feel like we have nothing under our control when our memory and emotions tend to have way too much control over us. Each person has a different trigger that drives them into oblivion, and then it becomes crucial to stop, reflect, and identify those triggers. Some people take this as a challenge, taking back control, but others are just too overwhelmed and struggle with negative beliefs.

To attract abundance and manifest your dreams, you must come first. There is nothing wrong with having negative thoughts. It is natural. The vital thing is to get back up with a bang! Ever wondered if you should have an exercise or process to evaluate your beliefs and find out which ones really support you and which ones pull you down?

It also becomes important to replace a negative belief that has been ingrained in your psyche for so long. The idea is to observe the negative thoughts from a distance while allowing the positive thoughts to resonate within you. When you observe your thoughts regularly and acknowledge the feelings behind them, you ultimately are able to identify and become aware of the ones that take away or enhance. Essentially, feelings provide us with valuable information and communication of our inner self. In order for us to experience positive feelings, we must first in build the new thought in our minds so that our bodies can start living them.

Facing extremely challenging situations that are ultimately unavoidable can lead to a positive shift in your mindset and emotions. The struggle can serve as a catalyst for personal growth and help you develop resilience and a stronger sense of self. By embracing the struggles of life, we can gain confidence in our individual strengths, which may increase our tolerance to that particular stressor. Sometimes, we don't have our full potential to tackle problems, but if we know what we're dealing with, we can do better. By doing and moving forward, we know that new possibilities for one's life may await.

Fighting:

Fighting has always been viewed as a negative regret and is generally associated with weakness. However, what many ignore is that these difficult experiences are a natural part of our lives and that these moments help us to grow. It is natural to have good times in your life, and it is natural to have bad times in your life too. There's nothing weak about continuing your struggles. It doesn't make you any less fragile than anyone else, and I would even say it makes you stronger.

Struggles Help Gain Experience:

Our struggles shape our moments as they strengthen us physically and mentally. Think about how a muscle is strengthened; it is constantly stressed and eventually rebuilt. Similarly, through a fight, we learn to think, breathe and deal optimally with stressful situations. When you view struggles as opportunities for personal growth and development, you are more likely to remain grounded and open-minded. You can approach these situations as chances to learn and improve rather than seeing them as threats to your ego or sense of self-worth. We sense different perspectives in life and build resistance to difficulties. The only way to gain experience in combat is to survive the battle. That's why this experience is a strength.

You Inspire and Encourage Others:

Motivating and inspiring others is a great strength. It's a powerful way of giving value to others. People naturally look to others who have experience. Fighting is interesting, and people can't help but pay attention to those who fought. Everyone wants to know the secret to overcome adversity and hear it from someone who has experienced it themselves. Troubled people can empower others by becoming leaders and mentors to others going through the same things. They would offer value in exchange for yours, and that makes the ability to inspire powerful.

They Help you Stay Calm and Collected:

Sudden changes cannot affect these people because they know that life can throw anything at them. What keeps them calm is the knowledge that they can get through it with confidence. Every struggle prepared her to go through life with ease. Much like fear is minimized by constant exposure, so is combat. Having the ability to be calm in stressful situations is a strong trait and can only be developed through combat.

Fighting Inspires a Sense of Urgency:

In this age, there are countless stories of people fighting them and going through rags to riches. Struggle compels people to act, and these acts of desperation can pave the way to one's goals and dreams. When you're desperate to survive and thrive, you make remarkable achievements. That desperation and urge to survive is a power not everyone can experience.

Help Find the Beauty in Life:

Being able, beautiful, and finding joy in undesirable situations is a gift and a strength. Every experience is painting for the canvas you call life. They know they can be happy at any time in their lives, and they use it to their advantage. You must first be willing to accept the challenge, understand it, and then try to overcome it because often when a problem arises, we tend to neglect it, which ends up making the problem even worse.

In a nutshell, struggles strengthen us and can create transformation, but that is only if we let them. There are quite a lot of problems in life that we need to overcome, and it is good that you have difficulties in your life. Life is meaningless without challenges because it helps you grow, and this type of learning prepares you for the next time. Everyone fights. It's as inevitable as breathing. While this might be true, there are those who struggle more than others. Fighting and responding to struggles makes people stronger. Every worthwhile achievement is built through fighting.

Chapter 3: Understanding Non-Productive Thoughts and the Inner Critic

I don't have what it takes...

I am not good enough...

I don't deserve to be loved...

I don't fit in...

I can't make a relationship work...

Do you come across these types of thoughts too? Does your mind trigger these destructive ideas in your brain too? Well, if you answered my questions in the affirmative, you're not alone.

Do you know that according to the National Science Foundation, our brain generates around 12,000 to 60,000 thoughts per day, and around 80% of those thoughts are negative? This means that out of all ideas we have throughout the day, 40 to 50 thousand of those thoughts are just negative. Certainly, that's a tedious task for anyone to shoo them away, isn't it? Because yes, we need to manage and filter those thoughts to ensure they don't make a home in our minds and slowly creep into our personality, turning us into something we are certainly not and taking us away from our performance! Once upon a time, you could get away with this damaging verbiage. But after years of continuous personal assault, your mind and body cannot take it anymore. We cannot perform at our best. As a result, we need to start a spirited campaign that we truly understand and believe. Confrontation is necessary because staying in the dark or shadows of regret may create harmful growth that will negatively impact our life performances.

The Performance of Life

The great performance is between you and only you. It's the performance of your life, and it belongs to you and you alone. You are the main character, and the experiences you have will bring both joy and sorrow, much like the Yin and Yang of life. While joy can keep us motivated to continue, it's the sorrows that challenge us the most and can cause us to hit the eject button altogether and stop performing. This is the great challenge in life: How do I handle the social-emotional pain that comes my way? It's a question we all must answer at some point, for the SHOW will go on whether you're ready or not.

Performance is something that every person can relate to, regardless of their profession or role in life. It's about striving to be the best version of yourself, whether you're a brain surgeon, CEO, firefighter, student, parent, or friend.

For a brain surgeon, it means executing complex

surgeries with precision and care. For a CEO, it means driving their company to success while balancing the needs of their employees and stakeholders. For firefighters, it means being prepared and ready to respond to emergencies with bravery and efficiency. For parents, it means providing love, support, and guidance to their children and creating a safe and nurturing environment for them to grow and thrive, and for friends, it means being there for each other through thick and thin.

Performance is also about everyday activities, such as being a loving and supportive parent, a dedicated student, or a dependable friend. It's about setting goals for yourself and working hard to achieve them, no matter how big or small they may be. It's about facing challenges with resilience and determination and learning from your mistakes to become a better version of yourself because, at the end of the day, *life is a performance.*

Here, I recall the story of the gardener here who one day noticed a small weed in his lovely garden but thought to leave it as is since he felt tired at that moment. The next day, he went away on a two-week trip, forgetting about the weed. When he returned from his journey, he saw his entire garden covered in weeds and his produce dead! As a gardener, how was his performance?

Don't you think telling yourself, *Maybe I am not good enough,* is really a big thing? You might not say that to yourself on a daily basis, but don't you think it is just like the small weed the gardener left in his garden? The point is, if we just let in one bad thought in our head and don't get rid of it, it will sprout. But it won't only sprout one weed but also kick start a series of negative feelings, overthinking, and made-up scenarios, and before you would know it, you will have too much to control, just like a whole garden of weeds and dead good feelings.

Most of the time, the negative thoughts we experience are erroneous representations of reality. To be precise, they are a result of faulty and negative thinking. Remember that almost everything that subsists in our minds - every sensation, thought, idea, or scenario - happens only in our own secluded internal world. Your thoughts exist only to you and are not perceived by anybody else. Only one physical world is present on Earth, but thousands and thousands of different internal worlds exist. We are all in our own distinct theaters, beholding completely different shows, and still, we act as if the audience outside knows about our internal show, viewing the exact same occurrence we call 'life.' Thoughts are not real. Whether it is a positive or negative idea depends on your perception and outlook.

Thoughts are either memories replaying themselves or fancies of the mind. Neither memory nor imagination is real. So, relax, take a deep breath, and know that you are the vacant screen upon which the thoughts play, just like the clouds that appear and vanish in the boundless sky.

The Inner Critic

When I say 'inner critic,' you know what I mean. Yes, that punitive voice in your head that prompts you of your shortfalls, slipups, and failures. The voice that deceitfully makes you question yourself and your dignity. The same voice that keeps you trapped and existing with relentless remorse, embarrassment, guilt, and distress, and the same voice that every so often starts chatting away at you without any invitation. You just can't stop it from expressing its opinion when you confront a challenge or take a risk, right? It bombards you with the vilest insults, and in worst-case scenarios, you end up questioning your entire being. Yes, that's what I am talking about, your 'inner critic.'

The inner critic is grounded in opinionated thoughts to take us down. It knows our weakness, goes for a kill shot every time, has no remorse, and does not want us or anyone else to succeed. The automatic thoughts it spews are founded on cognitive distortions and are not factual.

Dr. Marilee Adams has termed this inner critic as the 'Judger.' And rightly so because this voice ends up doing nothing but judging us, often time destructively than constructively, and consequently knocks us down emotionally. In due course, this voice impacts our minds so much that we get dragged down a bottomless pit of 'judgments.' According to research,[1] individuals who criticize themselves more have been observed to be in a state of low mood, which triggers more inner criticisms, further declining the spirit.

Self-criticism can turn out to be a crucial characteristic of people's relationship with themselves. It is essential to know that it usually shoots from our learned behaviors. For example, chasing academic or work brilliance may have directed you to an inevitable inner critic, or maybe you put a wasteful amount of pressure on yourself to be in a relationship. In the end, your self-worth and self-respect suffered, which taxed your psychological well-being. It is essential to mention here that not only this nasty voice in our heads impacts our psychological well-being, but it also disrupts performance and productivity in different life arenas, be it at work, in sports, in academics, in social settings, in family relationships, or in religion.

Doubt and self-criticism never lead us onto the road

to success. As Henry Ford said, *"W*hether you think you can or you can't -you're right. *"* What do you think that means? It shows that the things we tell ourselves and believe in are how we interpret the world, which serves as a lens through which we look. What we see, experience, ponder, and sense are all attuned over this lens which ultimately results in how we live our lives. But often, we can't stop the negative inner dialogue in our minds and spiral down a self-deprecating route.

Let me make it easier for you. Consider two people at your workplace. One makes quick decisions and is confident about what he does. On the other hand, the second person often doubts what he does and mostly questions himself. Who do you think is likely to move ahead in their careers at a swift speed? Well, if you ask me, the world we live in demands rational reasoning and quick decision-making powers. In reality, individuals whose inner critic is switched 'on' quite often find it challenging to be productive since their cognitive processes are slackened under stress. So, the second guy, due to being caught in the vicious cycles of the inner critic, would thus, hesitate since he doesn't believe in himself, which gives the inner critic more power and causes him to be more fearful. Second guessing himself would lead him to missed opportunities since he wouldn't focus on if he has what it takes, rather than going for it and trusting himself. So, the first guy has more potential to move ahead since he has confidence under his belt about his performance and his perception of the work he did.

As humans, we want to operate out of power rather than fear. Engaging in internal self-criticism can impede our cognitive processing as we struggle with the ongoing dialogue within ourselves, leading to reduced productivity. Because when we listen to a constant voice targeting our self-esteem, we get demoted, not only at work but also in studies, sports, and our personal relationships. For instance, you might even stop making friends because you're worried about what they will think about you. You might go to a party, try to interact, and then instantly, the inner critic would pop up on your shoulder and whisper, *"Oh, my God. Did I say the right thing?"* That's what stabs our power to believe in ourselves. At times, it might appear as if your negative judgments are protecting you or even keeping you 'down-to-earth,' but what they are actually doing is holding you confined in a disparaging cycle of pressure and subsequent gloom.

Have you heard about ANTs? Or let me first say, have you ever heard about ants spoiling a picnic? Well, the ANTs I am talking about can end up spoiling your life.

Aaron Beck, MD, is known as the founder of Cognitive Behavioral Therapy, commonly known as CBT. Back in the 1960s, Beck worked with patients suffering from depression and observed that streams of negative thoughts impulsively appeared. He became persuaded that involuntary negative feelings and judgments such as "I can never succeed" or "I am good at nothing" affected general contentment and psychological well-being and even instigated the condition of his patients. He observed that their negative, partisan rationale fell into three classes: bad notions about themselves, the world, and the future. So, he termed these thoughts 'Automatic Negative Thoughts' and granted them the notable acronym of *ANTs*.

With each performance in life, our mind can convince us of something totally false. The mind dupes us into thinking that our undesirable views are precise and reasonable; however, in actual fact, they assist only in underpinning negative ideas and feelings, tanking our show.

The actual purpose of our total views is to aid us in making sense of our experiences. Nonetheless, they can turn out to be fruitless or even damaging later in life.

For instance, you may tell yourself you are not worthy of love or are wicked, useless, ugly, senseless, or existentially imperfect in many ways. Our inner critics continuously transmit these messages and ideas into our brains. And as we strive to improve our performance in various aspects of our lives, our inner critics can become more vocal. Despite our best efforts, we may find ourselves returning to these challenging beliefs, which can hinder our growth and progress in the performance of life in different roles.

Cognitive Behavior Therapy

Cognitive behavioral therapy is a therapeutic approach that has been shown as an effective treatment for depression, anxiety disorders, and other mental health conditions. CBT is one of the most heavily researched types of therapy, and study after study has found it equally as effective, if not more effective, than many other mental health treatments. In fact, CBT stands out from the crowd since there is abundant empirical evidence that it produces long-term change for people who struggle with mental illness.

Cognitive behavioral therapy is based on the idea that many psychological challenges are partly due to unhelpful thinking and behavior patterns. The CBT model emphasizes that the results of our emotions and behaviors are directly influenced by how we perceive events. Essentially, it is not the specific event that is the determining factor in how one feels, but rather, it is the individual's interpretation and internalization of the proceeding event.

CBT treatment focuses on teaching people to challenge these unhelpful patterns, making it easier to cope with their condition. The idea is that while we can't change our circumstances when difficult situations come up, we can change how we react to them. You can understand CBT in a personal manner as well. For instance, we may contemplate it as the course of rewriting our stories in life.

Through performances, each of us has a unique life story comprising events, feelings, lessons, and expectations. It has, in one way or the other, transformed us into becoming who we are today, the way we handle life situations, and how we assume life to disclose in the forthcoming. Remember that CBT isn't a time-traveling device since it obviously could not let you alter the incident itself, but it changes the way you think about it or responds to similar life situations.

We can't transform the past, but then again, we can definitely change our thinking about it.

Cognitive Behavioral Theory is more about changing how you write your life story instead of what is already penned down in your mind. The procedure of inscribing your life story is mainly passive, even though people undeniably put their own twist on memories (every so often, deliberately). We are inclined not to heed how we record, repeat, narrate and retort to our life stories. We are typically absorbed in the content. CBT assists us in becoming more conscious of how our 'writing style' influences the incident in our mind, letting us get more involved in the procedure of writing our story.

Our behaviors are intertwined directly with our cognitions (psychological paradigms like thoughts, sentiments, and recollections). These perceptions subsidize the development of our life stories. Mental health can agonize due to indiscretions in creating and operating these cognitive processes. For instance, you may have developed an illogical fear of dogs due to a bad childhood experience. The fear might have developed over time because you left it unexamined. Your life story might probably be enclosed in a negative light every time a dog is involved in it. CBT could aid you in detecting your fear's source, in this case, the first dog incident, and sooner or later, getting rid of it with proven treatment methods. You would then be able to reconsider your former experiences related to dogs from a new-fangled standpoint, which will allow you to reword your life story.

Let me give you another example here. One night, a man is woken up by a loud thud in his house. The noise came from downstairs, which was so loud that it woke him up. The man thinks it is a burglar who broke into the house at night. What do you think he would feel or do? An opinion is that he might feel fear or an urge to hide due to the thoughts of being robbed. Alternatively, he might also feel angry and try to confront the burglar.

Now take the same circumstances but with a little twist. This time, the man recalls having a cat and leaving the kitchen window open. What do you think his behavior would be this time? Considering that it might be the cat may only make him a little annoyed or distressed, and at most, he might just go down and close the window.

This example demonstrates how our judgments, state of mind, and actions are meticulously interrelated. It correspondingly indicates that the problem is not so much about our life events but how we infer them. Our thoughts and emotions are interconnected and can have a significant impact on our mental well-being. While it is normal to experience negative emotions such as anger or sadness, it is often our own thoughts and actions that reinforce and amplify these feelings. For example, if we constantly dwell on perceived injustices and mistreatment by others, our anger and resentment towards them can grow stronger over time. Similarly, if we repeatedly focus on the positive qualities of a person we are attached to, our attachment can become more intense.

This highlights the power of our own minds in shaping our emotional experiences. By becoming aware of our thought patterns and actively working to shift our focus towards more positive or productive thoughts, we can potentially alleviate some of the mental unrest and suffering we experience.

Whether you suffer from anxiety, depression, lack of self-esteem, or self-confidence, or have undergone a traumatic event that made you rethink and reevaluate your life a hundred times a day, you can get back on track and achieve the love, comfort, and peace you deserve and long crave for. I wouldn't say the journey would be easy, but the first step in the process is what we are talking about – CBT. Let me put it this way. Deep inside of you, there is a garden thick with countless seeds.

But among all those seeds, three very special seeds have names: confidence, calmness, and contentment.

You were born with them, but when you were little, the garden was not looked after, and the seeds of horrid weeds started to invade your seeds of confidence, calmness, and contentment. As you grew, you assumed the weeds had taken over the garden and that confidence, calmness, and contentment were slayed.

Gone forever. Vanished into thin air.

What you are unaware of is that the petite seeds, no matter how often they were crushed or abandoned, are the stoutest seeds in your garden. They are active, only lying latent for several years. When you would start cultivating the garden yourself by nurturing the seeds with the love and reverence they deserve, trivial yet strong, pretty shoots will begin to grow.

Soon, they will dispel the weeds and turn out to be the most gorgeous flowers in your garden. In due course, they will sow other seeds into the lush and rich soil of your heart, which will eventually flourish with lovely flowers such as hope, harmony, and dignity. Nobody will be able to tread in your garden and crush your beautiful seeds again because you won't let them!

Cognitive Distortions

We talked about cognitive distortions briefly earlier in the chapter. Now, let me explain in a bit more detail since, all in all, this is where it all sums up.

The human brain naturally wants to form connections. Most of the time, this is helpful for teaching us how to interact with the world. Sometimes, however, we create relationships between things that don't exist to our detriment. For example, if you fail at something, your brain may think, *"I will never be successful,"* which is both unhelpful and untrue. Essentially these thoughts are automatic and influence one's emotions, behavior, and physiological response.

Cognitive distortions are all irrational and false and may cause us psychological harm. In her book *Cognitive Therapy: Basics and Beyond*[2], Dr. Judith Beck identified specific, common cognitive distortions, some of which we have outlined below. The countless negative feelings we have throughout the day are not true depictions of reality or our personalities. Instead, they might be a result of faulty thinking. Catastrophizing, sweeping statements, all-or-nothing thoughts, and mixing our sentiments with facts are just some ways we persuade ourselves of something false or erroneous.[3] Mistaken and negative insights about ourselves and our experiences can direct us down a deep hole of negative thinking that might feel out of our control. Also, as per a study, cognitive distortions have been found to be associated with the development of psychopathology[4], and they can increase the conspicuous undesirable judgments along with delaying problem-solving and diminishing cognitive flexibility[5].

A large non-clinical population, approximately 80% to 99%, experiences bad thoughts. When these patterns turn out to be critical and self-defeating and begin to hinder a person's happiness, they must be paid heed to and resolved. We talked about Automatic Negative Thought Patterns, remember? Well, cognitive distortions are an integral part of it. As I said earlier, cognitive biases and distortions fool us into thinking that whatever thoughts we are having is the actual truth, whereas they only reinforce negative thinking patterns. Let us talk about these cognitive biases.

Black-and-White Thinking

Black-and-white thinking, also known as all-or-nothing thinking or polarized thinking, is thinking in terms of extremes. There are no shades of gray with black-and-white thinking. You are either perfect or a complete failure; your life is either fantastic or absolutely terrible. Essentially, you view situations in two categories instead of on a continuum.

Catastrophic Thinking

This is the type of thinking that endues the worst-case scenarios. You view the future negatively without examining evidence that contradicts its appraisals, which is known as catastrophizing.

Over Generalization

This is when you take one instance and develop a conclusion that goes far beyond the current situation in view. For example, you might get a "D" on a test and take this to mean that you cannot be a good employee at the local restaurant.

Mind Reading

You may make assumptions about what a person is thinking, why they behave the way they do, and how they feel about you without asking if you are correct.

Disqualifying the Positive

When you disqualify the positive, you may acknowledge a positive experience but reject it. For example, if someone gives you a compliment, you might attribute it to them trying to get on your good side and having nothing to do with your own positive qualities.

Magnification/Minimization

We minimize all the great things happening to us, and we maximize all the bad. Completely lopsided in favor of the negative.

Should Statements

You can recognize this distortion by the words 'should,' 'must,' and 'ought.' These are rules for behavior that you adopt for yourself and others. When you don't live up to these rules, you feel guilty, and when others don't, you feel angry at them. Remember, 'shoulds' can cause frustration, resentment, and guilt.

Emotional Reasoning

With emotional reasoning, you believe that because you feel something, it must be true despite contradictory evidence. Whatever unhealthy feeling you have reflects who you are as a person.

Personalization

We blame ourselves for others behaving negatively. For example, *the boss was short with me because I must have done something wrong.* We fail to recognize other possible explanations for their behavior. It's possible that the reason behind the boss's behavior is a painful divorce they are currently going through.

Core Beliefs

Beginning in early childhood, individuals start to

develop certain beliefs about themselves, others, and their world. Core beliefs inspire our behaviors, emotions, thinking patterns, and perceptions based on thoughts. These are the physical, emotional, and mental levels. Our belief system, while invisible, is plotting the trajectory of our life; it is 'being activated' moment-to-moment by the world in view.

Core beliefs, as opposed to peripheral beliefs, underlie the rest of the belief system. They support the peripheral beliefs as a basis for them.

They make it *possible* to have those peripheral views. I can't believe that *"I'm a bad worker"* if I don't first hold the core belief "I am a worker." Our belief system plays a significant role in shaping our lives, and our core beliefs are at the heart of this system. When we acknowledge the powerful impact that our belief system has on our daily lives, we begin to see how our core beliefs play a central role in shaping our perceptions of reality. By recognizing the influence of our core beliefs, we can start to understand how they shape our thoughts, emotions, and behaviors and impact our overall performance and success in life.

It takes a lot of power to ask yourself, *"What are my core beliefs?"* or *"Are they really true?"* For, if a core belief is shaken, then the whole structure resting on that foundation can collapse. It is not necessary to take apart each belief, but one by one, you can *strike at the root* to make sure you comprehend them and realize the truth.

Thus, not only is it important to comprehend our negative thinking patterns, cognitive distortions, and our core beliefs, but also work on them and try to combat the inner critic and ANTs to bring out the best in ourselves! Else, the negative sentiments won't only ruin your happiness but also make sure to wither away every inch of peace within you until you are nothing but dry, barren land.

Have you heard the famous story of the two wolves? I have that short story framed in my office and often use it with my clients. I am not very sure about the story's origin, but this ancient anecdote has been part of the Native American generations for years, and why not? It's so deep and amazing. If you haven't heard about it, let me narrate it for you, and if yes, let me do it anyway so you get reminded of the message we are bringing home!

One evening an old Cherokee told his grandson about a battle that was going on inside himself. He said, *"My son, it is between two wolves. One is evil: anger, envy, sorrow, regret, greed, arrogance, self-pity, guilt, resentment, inferiority, lies, false pride, superiority, and ego. The other is good: joy, peace, love, hope, serenity, humility, kindness, benevolence, empathy, generosity, truth, compassion, and faith."*

The grandson thought about it for a minute and then asked his grandfather, *"Which wolf wins?"*

The old Cherokee simply replied, *"The one I feed."*

Well, ask yourself then, which wolf are *YOU* feeding?

Chapter 4: The Rebirth and Reframe

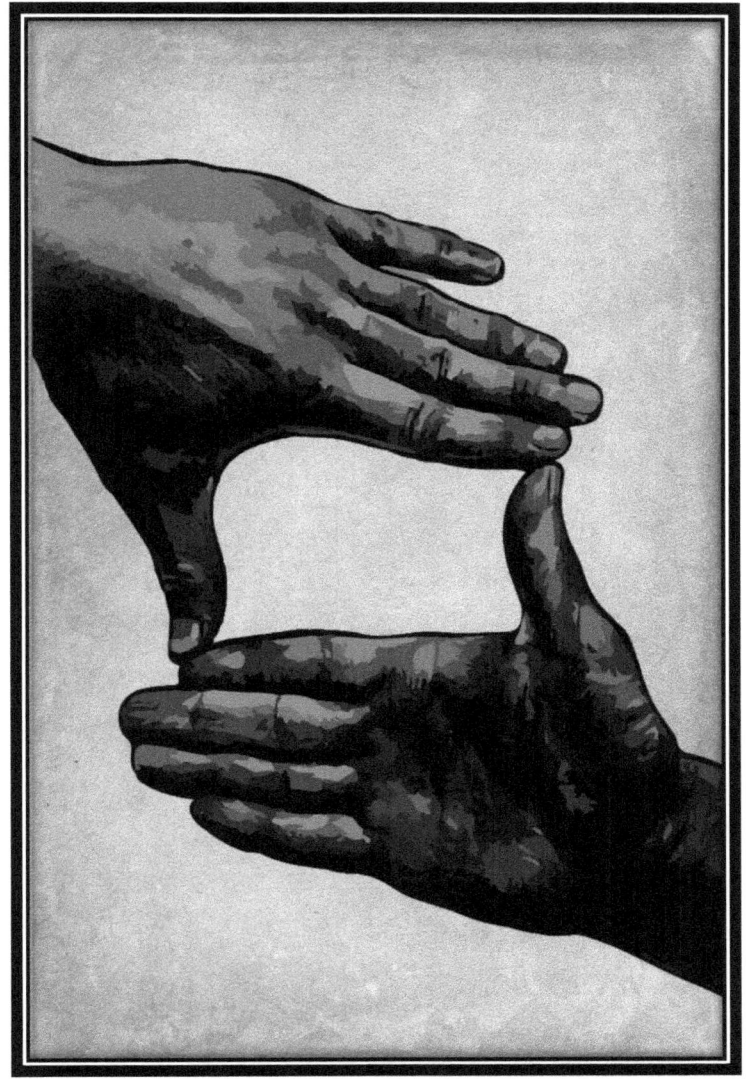

"Life's essence lies not in what befalls you, but in the power, you wield to shape its course through the choices you make and the way you respond."

Rebirth, the concept of starting anew, has been an idea that has fascinated humans for centuries. The idea that we can shed our past, learn from our mistakes, and begin again with a fresh start has been the inspiration for countless works of literature, art, and music. But what is it about the idea of rebirth that is so appealing? And how can it motivate us to achieve our goals and become the best versions of ourselves?

First and foremost, the concept of rebirth is inherently tied to the idea of a comeback story. We all love a good underdog tale where the protagonist overcomes incredible odds and emerges victorious. The idea taps into this desire for a redemption story, where we can leave behind our failures and emerge triumphant. When we embrace the idea of rebirth, we are giving ourselves permission to start again, to wipe the slate clean, and to move forward with a renewed sense of purpose.

Rejuvenation is the exhilarating byproduct of the rebirth experience. By fully embracing the idea of a fresh start, we also commit ourselves to a powerful journey of self-improvement and personal growth. It's a time to shed our old skin and rise from the ashes, stronger and more resilient than ever before. We may be leaving behind our past mistakes and failures, but we are also coming off our old selves and becoming someone new. This process of rebirth allows us to decide what we want to carry forward and what we want to leave behind. We can set new goals, create new habits, and redefine ourselves in a way that is more aligned with our values and aspirations.

One of the most powerful aspects of the rebirth concept is the way it encourages us to focus on our internal selves. Rather than looking for external validation or success, we are encouraged to turn inward and focus on our own growth and development. This inside-out approach allows us to cultivate a stronger sense of self-awareness, self-acceptance, and self-love. By embracing this idea, we are actually giving ourselves permission to be imperfect, to make mistakes, and to learn from them. We are also embracing the idea that true success and happiness come from within and not from external factors.

The rebirth concept marks the ultimate demise of our former selves and the rise of a new, improved version of ourselves. It's clear that it holds tremendous potential for personal transformation. By recognizing that we have the power to let go of our old identities and start fresh, we can tap into a wellspring of motivation and inspiration to pursue our dreams and live our best lives.

As we embrace this concept and the potential for self-evolution it offers, we can begin to imagine a life where hope is not just a distant possibility but a tangible reality. Have you ever thought about what life would be like if we lived inside hope? Not admire it from a distance, contemplating to have it but living right in it, under its roof? Well, life is much easier when that happens because I know that we can see the stars only when it is dark enough. Similarly, we can live under hope when we believe in our heart, *"This is exactly what I aspire to in life!"*

One thing I strongly believe in life is that it's all in our brains, no matter if it's happiness, sadness, anger, fear, anticipation, surprise, or disgust. It's all the wiring in our brain that forms the reactions we give to a situation or feel about them. As C. JoyBell C. once said, *"Happiness is a choice."*

But you would say, *"It's not that easy, Trent. It's not that easy."* Well, I believe you are right, but it's a good thing to give it a thought, no? Quite frankly, it is what we actually talk about in Cognitive Behavioral Therapy.

As we discussed in Chapter 3, CBT is based on the idea that our thoughts, as opposed to events, impact our emotions and, ultimately, behavior. Your feelings are determined by what happens and your perception of what happened.

To understand better, let's say you were invited to a party where you didn't know anyone. The way you think about the invitation will impact the way you feel about it.

You might think, *"That sounds fun! I would love to meet new people."* This thought will trigger a happy and exciting feeling.

On the other hand, you might think, *"That doesn't sound like my idea of fun. I would rather stay in."* This type of thought might give a neutral feeling.

However, you can also experience a third type of thought, such as, *"That sounds like my nightmare! I feel too awkward around new people."* This way of thinking will make you anxious and upset.

You can see through this example that the same event can have a profoundly different impact on different people based on their perceptions. Have you ever taken photos of a Sunflower or any other flower? One thing photography makes us understand is how, by changing the camera angle a little, a completely different scenario comes into view.

There might be a humble bunch of sunflowers sitting on your kitchen slab. You click a picture of it such that only the flower comes into view. Now, you pull back the camera a little and take your kitchen slab and kitchen door into the frame too. By pulling back and including the surrounding of the sunflowers, put your tall vase of sunflowers into another context - a contented little blossom on a cold, gray day.

Now, if you would zoom into the camera and take a closer shot of the central flower of the sunflower, minute details of the flower would come into view and tell you a whole different story of a completely new world of possibilities.

Then, if you take your camera to the stem side and take a picture of the flower's underneath part (an often-overlooked perspective), you will discover a unique side with an exceptional beauty of its own. Not to forget the fact that sunflowers can grow up to 6ft tall, but we usually only see it from the top or a closer side angle that makes it look smaller.

Thus, that's the power of perspective. How each of those pictures (of the same single flower) tells an entirely different story, not to forget that one picture (one perspective) does not negate the other, and individually, each picture alone does not convey the entire story.

Have you wondered how often we do this in our lives? How often do we perceive things from one standpoint only? And when we are confronted with an incompatible perspective, how do we try to resolve it with our own particular experience?

It is important to understand that life is not really very different from sunflowers. And photography teaches us to appreciate the little things and big things equally through the angles we choose to view things and our approach. So, if you don't like how something is at this moment, just change the angle. Our emotions are influenced by our beliefs, attitudes, and expectations. For instance, people with anxiety experience negative thoughts that contribute to their feelings of anxiety and fear. Cognitive behavioral therapy aims to identify negative thought patterns to ease anxious thoughts. By challenging these thoughts in cognitive behavioral therapy, people with anxiety can change the way they feel.

Cognitive Restructuring

Cognitive restructuring, also known as thought challenging, is a central aspect of cognitive behavioral therapy. It is the procedure by which particular reasonings are treated as hypotheses instead of facts and studied within the framework of all pertinent data rather than just the information that is subtly available via different cognitive processes. It is a very successful process, and research reveals that CBT is the most effective treatment method for people dealing with depression and anxiety.

The main idea of this approach is to challenge our negative thought patterns that cause anxiety and replace them with more realistic and optimistic thoughts. Let us take a deeper look into this process, consisting of three steps.

- **Identify the Negative Thought**

Anxiety makes things seem more dangerous than they truly are. For example, a person with a germ phobia may be too frightened to touch another person because they worry, they will die.

This thought is irrational, but it's easier to say this because we look at it from an outsider's perspective. When the anxious thoughts are our own, it is more difficult to challenge them and, most of all, identify them in the first place. But that's where it all starts - acknowledging our disruptive ideas and behaviors.

- **Challenge the Negative Thought**

Once the negative thoughts are identified, it's time to evaluate them. CBT takes a scientific approach to challenge these thoughts. You start by considering the evidence of your negative thought and questioning them, analyzing negative beliefs, considering the pros and cons of your worries, and analyzing how realistic your fears are.

- **Replacing the Negative Thought with a Realistic One**

Once you identify and challenge the negative thought, it's time to replace it with a more realistic and positive idea. You come up with calming statements you can rely on to repeat to yourself when entering an anxiety-ridden situation.

So, in a nutshell, we need to explore the origin of a distressing feeling and how it may arise from an irrational belief. The therapist then helps the client to challenge the irrational belief and replace it with a rational one and may send you home with worksheets to write down other irrational beliefs and possible alternatives that will produce better feelings.

Let's say you have social anxiety and a wedding to go to where you only know the bride. You are terrified to go because you are too nervous that you will be awkward around a large group of new people. You think that you will embarrass yourself and other people will judge you. So, in order to work on your thoughts following the CBT process, write down your negative thoughts about the wedding, identify the distortions in your thinking, and come up with a more realistic thought to replace them.

Let me give you another example here. You made a mistake at work. The mistake wasn't too big, but your boss asked you to be careful in the future. Now, the blunder is making you think about the worst-case scenarios.

You come home, get fresh and sit on your bed. The first thought you have is, *'I don't belong in this organization.'*

In this case, your belief system can work in two different ways.

1. *It's horrible! It's a devastating tragedy if my manager pointed out a mistake I made. I won't ever be able to provide for my family.* (Irrational)
2. *It's a little disappointing that my toxic boss reminded me to be careful in the future rather than appreciating the things I did right.*

The resulting feeling from belief number 1 can make you feel horrible, hurt, rejected, and lacking in human value.

Belief number 2 might result in an annoying feeling.

So here comes the 'disputation.' You might want to stop for a moment and ask yourself, *"Am I jumping to a conclusion?"* or maybe give a thought to in what way did the manager say those words to you? Were they meant to be a reminder, or were they meant to be hurting? (Remember, there is a fine line between mentoring/training and degrading an employee). Thus, a better solution in this situation would be to have a talk with your manager and tell him you will be careful in the future and that you will try to be productive. At the end of the day, mistakes, hard work, and consistency are what makes us progress in our career and life as a whole.

Let's take a deeper look into the 'challenging negative thoughts' exercise.

Challenging Negative Thoughts Exercise

We need to uninstall our program, for it no longer benefits us. Cognitive restructuring is about pressing, pausing, resetting, and molding your thoughts into balanced ones without overthinking.

The following are some examples to help you understand the process.

Negative Thought: *I'm going to be so embarrassed attending this wedding by myself. I won't be able to function appropriately.*

Distortion: Fortune telling - catastrophizing.

Realistic Replacement Thought: *The focus isn't going to be on me. This is a joyous moment for everyone. It is okay to be me.*

Negative Thought: *I'm going to embarrass myself at the wedding. As a result, I don't have the ability to be a good manager.*

Distortion: Overgeneralization

Realistic Replacement Thought: *These two events are NOT related at all. If anything, use your managerial skills and win people over.*

Negative Thought: *Everyone is going to think I am an awkward loser.*

Distortion: Mind Reading

Realistic Replacement Thought: *Everyone just wants to have a fun time at a wedding. You are not the focus of this wedding.*

Conquering a lifetime of a certain negative thought pattern doesn't happen overnight. The key is repeated efforts to break this habit. As per the Italian proverb, *"Dripping water hollows out stone, not through force but through persistence."* Honestly, that is what it is all about – persistence. Keep on trying, and you will get the results, just like the blacksmith who forges steel over and over, repeating the same process again and again. But the end result is a seasoned sword that is stronger and cuts through anything in battle. The same is the case with Cognitive Restructuring, which is also a repetitive process. You might feel it is not working out at one point or that your negative thought patterns keep bouncing back but continue to make efforts, and your consistency and persistence will work out.

Forge your negative thoughts into positive ones, like the blacksmith forges the steel, resulting in a unique piece of art that is strong enough to fight any battle. Similarly, going through cognitive restructuring, you will be seasoned and prepared to charge through the challenges in life and come out of them stronger than before. At the end of the day, it is all about persistence.

Remember the story of Colonel Sanders, the founder of KFC? At the age of 65, Colonel Sanders, with a shabby car and a $100 check from Social Security, apprehended he had to do something. He recalled the recipe his mother taught him, made the fried chicken, and went out selling. Guess how many doors he knocked on before getting his first order? It is projected that he had knocked on over 1000 doors before he got his first order.

Now think for a moment. How many of us give up after two tries, seven tries, fifty tries, or maybe at most a hundred tries? And then we sit and say, *I tried as hard as I could.* Quite a lesson of persistence for us all, isn't it?

Placebo Effect

Imagine you woke up in the middle of the night and felt an abrupt, strident pain in your neck. You lay still on the bed for some time, thinking it would go away, but the pain stays. You begin to move your neck and still feel a sharp ache. Your mind starts to trigger different thoughts. Now, you are worried. *What is happening? Am I sick? Is there something inside my neck? Is there a serious problem?* You end up deciding to visit the doctor first thing in the morning.

The following day you sit impatiently in the waiting room of your doctor's office and hold tight, anticipating and preparing yourself to hear about a serious problem with your neck. Then, you see the doctor coming out of his office. He greets you warmly, scrutinizes you, and comforts you that all is okay. Almost instantly, your dread and hurt improve. You may not realize it at this point, but you have just experienced the 'placebo effect.'

There are hundreds of ways our minds impact our lives, one of which is the placebo effect. The knowledge that you are being taken care of and provided medical assistance can make you feel better. This phenomenon is called the placebo effect. The brain has a remarkable ability to blur the lines between reality and imagination, and this phenomenon plays a significant role in the placebo effect. Essentially, when we visualize or imagine something happening, our brain processes it as if it were actually occurring in the physical world. This, in turn, triggers the release of various chemicals and neurotransmitters in the brain that serve to confirm the reality of the imagined experience.

The placebo effect, which occurs when a person experiences a positive response to a treatment that has no active ingredients, is a prime example of this phenomenon. Placebos work because the brain responds to the belief that the treatment is effective, regardless of whether or not it actually is.

Understanding the power of the mind-body connection is critical to improving our overall health and well-being. By harnessing the brain's ability to blur the lines between reality and imagination, we can potentially use our thoughts and beliefs to positively impact our physical and mental health.

You shouldn't think that Placebos would lower your blood pressure level or shrink a tumor. Rather, placebos work on symptoms controlled by the mind, such as pain perception. There are several diverse types of placebos. You might be acquainted with placebo medicines containing non-medicinal elements such as sugar or starch. Scientists frequently use placebos while testing the impacts of an innovative treatment or drug. They often give half of the study participants the active medicine and later compare the result to those who were given placebo pills. If there's more development in the experimental drug group when the experiment or study has been completed, researchers conclude that the cure or drug is effective. It is important to note here that Placebos don't necessarily come in the form of a pill. They can be a short story, healing techniques, acupuncture, etc.

All these methods can result in constructive effects on the body without any active medication. Let me give you another example of how powerful and profound impact our thoughts play in not only our psychological but also our physical well-being.

Back in 2002, a study shook the orthopedic world. Physicians and scholars formed a group of 180 patients suffering from joint pain and executed a surgical procedure on half of the participants. On the other hand, a 'fake' surgery was performed on the other half of the group. Real skin incisions were part of the fake surgery, so the participants didn't guess that the procedure performed on them was fake. After both the real and fake surgeries, both groups conveyed the same level of pain relief, which revealed that the placebo technique was just as effective as the surgery.[6]

Our thoughts are the most high-powered, passionate, and dominant tool we can harness for all stages of feat in life. Our mind shapes our personality, including who we are in the present and who we will turn out to be in the forthcoming, inducing our physical health as well as emotional state. The mind power is a tool we are still determining and just starting to unbridle. Our competence is far better and superior compared to what most of us can even instigate to visualize.

Your outlook is one of the most potent forces pushing you either away or towards attaining your goals and becoming a better version of yourself. With this information comes 'choice,' and choice brings along 'effort.' The effort is undoubtedly the toughest in the initial stage. Don't think you are a failure or can't manage anything on your own if you need to ask for help. It is okay. We are all humans. In actual fact, go ahead and do it. This may mean asking an acquaintance, coworker, counselor, or family member to hold you accountable or check in frequently. You can also choose to join a group of people where everyone is working toward a similar goal. You might choose to work on your thoughts, behavior, and thinking patterns on your own too. Just select the structure that works precisely for you and begin to harness the power of your mind.

Imposter Syndrome

Do you ever feel that all you have, all you accomplished, or all you did is just a fraud...that one day, you would be 'exposed'...that you don't deserve to be at the success level you are today, and that really, it's a question of when, not if, your true insufficiencies will be discovered by everyone around you?

These feelings are what we call 'Imposter syndrome' that prowls within almost all of us. It is just about a universal feeling for every person, even the apparently most self-assured of leaders, irrespective of age, gender, or business.

Our accomplishments are simply sacked as luck instead of proof of our ability, diligence, or proficiency. Nonetheless, this self-criticism has a perturbing secondary effect. The dread of "being exposed" breeds concern and is linked with greater levels of cortisol (the stress hormone) in the brain and body. Together with this, the emotional state of "not deserving" is associated with low levels of the 'neurotransmitter serotonin' (the mood driver) and low levels of dopamine, which are linked to reward and enthusiasm. Remarkably, regardless of whether you are a man or a woman, the lesser your poise, the lesser your testosterone levels, meaning you are less likely to yield healthy risks like getting a promotion at work. So, all things considered, by thinking this way, you are enlisting yourself for a cold chemical cocktail of terror, disgrace, hesitation, and wariness that leads to self-sabotage. Do you really think you need that in your life? I really hope your answer is NO!

When we struggle with self-doubt, no matter how consciously or subconsciously, we project all types of messages out to the world that gesture the eventual deal-breaker: mistrust. Think for a moment, if you don't trust yourself (self-belief), why should anyone else trust you? Why would anyone want to collaborate with you if you feel the need to proclaim yourself gratuitously? These signs are projected and retorted to in split-second timing by the minute brain parts called the amygdala, the earliest, intuitive brain part. When person qualm themselves, their feelings and thoughts get communicated down at an intensely primal level.

So here, the question that comes into view is: *how can I offset imposter syndrome and create my inner self-belief to communicate a trustworthy and comforting sense in my own skin?*

Well, we know that neuroplasticity, the brain's capability to form new trials and networks, has taught us that our underlying feelings and habits transform only by doing things differently and practicing thinking in innovative ways. And there, the initial step is becoming conscious of the impulse of self-doubt that makes us think, *"There are so many other people who deserve it more than me,"* or *"I am not up to this challenge!"*

Then, we need to downgrade the significance of these thoughts - think of them as psychological 'noise' that you do not need to pay heed to. At last, the final thing we must do is take action regardless of self-doubt. Recurrently practicing this approach will change the way you think as time passes. In a nutshell, there is no substitute for action. All imposter syndrome wants is to keep you trapped in a tight bubble you won't ever burst. Don't let it accomplish its goal.

Dealing With Your Inner Critic

Be it the placebo effect or imposter syndrome, both show how our mind plays games and affects every aspect of our lives. Without a doubt, they are a part of the inner critic we talked about in detail in the last chapter. It's all because of that perfectionistic voice within us that seems to enjoy reminding us, *"Hey, man. You're just not good enough."*

To combat this inner voice, we first need to acknowledge that having this voice inside our heads is completely normal. If you think you are 'abnormal' or have no 'self-worth' because of the voice inside your head, the fact of the matter is that a critical voice exists in each one of us. The more important thing is not to let it stay in the driver's seat constantly. Instead of despising the inner critical voice, wishing it would disappear, or interpreting it as a sign of low self-esteem, we must recognize that societal pressures reinforce our tendency to perceive threats and compare ourselves to others. By acknowledging the universality of the inner critic and understanding its influence on our thoughts and behaviors, we can take steps to limit its power over us and cultivate a more positive, self-affirming inner dialogue. Practicing to acknowledge this reality would result in less of our time going into fact denial, and more of it would go into favorably and rationally retorting to the inner judge.

We need to act opposite to the inner critic. The inner critic should not be silenced or ignored, but it must be answered. Replying to a negative inner voice with another negative voice is likely to increase frustration and inner conflict, strengthening the inner critic.

Many people have an extremely noxious relationship with their inner critic, either feeling hatred for it or associating all their successes with it. Well, none of the two approaches is suitable or helpful. What *does* help is admitting that the inner critic is part of your brain's core hardwiring (helping in contesting hatred feelings) while *correspondingly* comprehending that it isn't the most reliable source (helping in challenging feelings of unaccommodating loyalty).

First, you might want to rename the inner critic and call it a different name. "Inner Critic" may appear to be an inherently severe name, and if you feel the same, give it another name,[7] something that sounds a little tenderer or kinder such as "The Disciplinarian" or "The Protector." Play around with names in your head and analyze what sounds best to you. Then, comprehend your inner critic's playing techniques and the buttons it likes to push and respond to it accordingly. Articulating what your inner critic says helps you to gain the skill to notice it from a distance progressively rather than blending it with its philosophies and beliefs.

(This is fundamentally the core of mindfulness, parenthetically, which is to *witness* your feelings and thoughts instead of conferring to them.)

After that, you can answer in a different way. With a lot of practice and analysis of how to respond to your 'disciplinarian,' maybe one day you will be able to say, *"Oh, hey, Mr. Critic. Welcome back to me. I see you are doing your job the best you can, but I am not in the mood to have a chat with you today. Please stop by later, or maybe just don't at all."* You can also say to yourself,

"Hah, I know you are wired to do this, my brain. Thanks for trying to keep me safe,"

"I know you are infusing these thoughts in my brain, Mr. Critic, don't hide." or

"Oh, wow! That's one creative story I have heard

from my inner critic in a while."

There is no "correct" or "incorrect" way to answer back to the inner critic. It is more about what helps you at the time you are having negative thoughts. You can also tell it to just "shut up!" or just be neutral, saying, "Yeah, my brain makes these scenarios often" approach. The best way to find out what works for you would be to experiment with some comebacks and see what helps you the most. The critical point is to develop the skill to notice the critic and answer it instead of taking what it articulates at face value.

Becoming someone who is less critical of yourself does not happen instantaneously or overnight. I am telling you this from experience. Just like you have to work out with consistency to see the results, you must practice this recurrently to reap the benefits. Obviously, it will take you some time to get used to these approaches to answer your inner critic, but over time, it will become a habit. Nonetheless, the key is consistency.

Consistency and repetition are indispensable when generating new neural pathways. Your characteristic tendencies are etched networks in your brain, just like a ski trail used repeatedly. It is easy and natural to trail the already established and paved path. Going off track is tough, and in the start, it is particularly challenging to cut a new path on hard ice, like your brain's established neural networks. After you travel down a new way for some time, a new-fangled course will start to form. In due course, you will be able to go down that new pathway without difficulty. That is exactly what transpires in your brain when you try to adopt a new behavior or practice a new thought pattern. New channels and furrows are formed, and the previously unacquainted way of being is soon developed as a norm. Consequently, you would know exactly how to treat that little Mr. Inner Critic inside your head.

Wasting your time thinking about the level of hate or love you have in your heart for your inner critic or pondering over how intensely you want your inner critic to go away is not the best way to invest your time, energy, and mental resources. Acknowledge its existence, get inquisitive about it so you can learn its tricks, and make efforts to develop your critic's counterpart, whether it is a voice that's more sympathetic, caring, or simply more genuine and truthful.

Nonetheless, is the inner voice the only thing that distracts us from our goals? Is it the only source that befuddles our minds and makes us compare ourselves to other people out there? Well, not really...

Chapter 5: The Noise

We have all been there…fixated in our own minds, stuck on a three-minute talk from four days ago. We repeat it incessantly. *My friend shouldn't have talked to me like that. I am always so kind to her.* We get stuck. The voice in our minds goes from an ally to a spiteful nag, just winding impractically over the same things repeatedly. This noise averts us from attaining what we want in life.

The inner chatter that is part of everyone's brain becomes even more clear at this point. You might not always be conscious of this mental noise because it has developed as a profoundly rooted habit and is well-thought-out, a natural and devoted part of life.

This inner noise is like a circumstantial background noise that never stops, from the moment we open our eyes in the morning to the moment we fall asleep at night. Frequently, it even hinders us from falling asleep. But when do we notice this mental noise and realize that it is quite disturbing?

When you need to concentrate on a specific activity, such as preparing for an important exam, projects at work, reading, solving problems, etc., at this time, you develop more awareness of the buzz and persistent flow of extraneous and typically impractical or distracting thoughts.

This is the mental noise. If the thoughts are positive, that's okay. Nevertheless, too often, negative thoughts revolve in our minds and strengthen tension, worry, annoyance, or interruption. One thing that you absolutely do not need is these thoughts.

Don't misconstrue me. Surely, thinking is a valuable and vital activity essential for resolving difficulties, examining, studying, developing, etc. Though every so often, our mind cannot be engrossed, and it wanders where it likes, inhabiting our attention with minor and insignificant matters, useless thinking that wastes our time and energy.

Will I pass the exam?

Will I graduate college?

Why hasn't my son called me yet?

What if I did not manage to turn in the project on time?

What should I wear for the annual party at work?

What if I get fired from my job?

What if it rains heavily?

What if I died today? Who will look after my family?

What would happen if my husband died in an

accident?

The list is endless. The incessant chatter keeps playing in the background right from the time we wake up or even before that until we hit the bed at night. It does not allow us to enjoy the present; it makes us unhappy, angry, restless, and anxious and hampers our ability to concentrate as well. For instance, you might constantly recall your past and dwell on the mistakes you made or worry about the future. This refrains you from enjoying the current moment. You cannot change the past nor have any physical control over the future. What you have in your hands is to make the best of the present moment.

Moreover, procrastination is another form of internal noise. The noise takes us away from our given strengths that make us unique and successful and makes us feel bad since we compare ourselves to others and become anxious. It derails us and questions our abilities. The noise is toxic. The inner noise also sometimes expresses itself through compulsive inner monologue, which disrupts the peace of mind and makes it busy with fidgety, and, every now and then, upsetting thoughts. You might start to compare yourself with prolific figures and think, "Oh my, I am never going to be like them." Mind you, you might not say it aloud in your head, but these kinds of thoughts infest the background of the mind. All this becomes extremely exhausting, making us unreasonable and lethargic. This relentless mental chatter also makes us lose opportunities because of inadequate attention to our surrounding activities. The mind is a valuable tool but also must be controlled. Wouldn't it have been extraordinary if we could just use the brain while studying, working, cooking, or doing tasks and then switch it off and enjoy inner peace? Switching off the mind forms a state of inner peace. We are not passive, inactive, or dull in that state, just in a state of peace. In point of fact, it is a state of heightened consciousness, strong understanding, and a sharp mind.

So, are there ways to get rid of this inner noise? Well, there certainly are.

Shutting Off the Inner Noise

Before starting, let's do a short experiment. Before reading any further, try to detach your mind from everything you are doing, every thought in your mind, and every task forward in the day. Try to stop that mental noise and evaluate if you can watch your mind in a detached manner. Close your eyes and do it now!

….

….

....

Did it work?

You might realize that the thought, *"I need to stop thinking,"* occupied your mind when you tried to detach your mind from thinking. This means you thought to stop thinking while still thinking. A few moments later, you may overlook that your main goal was to watch your thoughts, and your mind will continue its ceaseless cerebral activity. This demonstrates how agitated the mind is and the lack of discipline it has. To quiet this chatter, several techniques are available, and different strategies work for different people in different situations. In a nutshell, it's all about the blend of strategies.

One of the strategies that can turn out helpful in this situation is your language. Research reveals that a humble strategy termed 'distanced self-talk' can let you shift your perspective and perceive problems more empirically. The primary thing you need to do is halt your inner noise from saying *"I, I, I"* and instead make use of some other terms or pronouns.

Think for a moment. Have you ever noticed how simple it seems to dish out advice to someone in need, yet when it comes to taking our own advice, we often fall short?

Well, surely language can be a powerful tool to help us coach ourselves through our problems as if we were speaking to another person.

By using our own name and non-first person pronouns, we can create some much-needed psychological distance from our problems. This newfound space allows us to view our challenges more objectively and offer ourselves constructive advice that we may have otherwise overlooked. It's almost like having a personal coach right there in our minds, guiding us through life's obstacles with a fresh perspective.

Self-distancing is a powerful technique that can help us overcome our own biases, assumptions, and emotional reactions to a problem. When we use our own name or third-person pronouns to refer to ourselves, we create a psychological distance that allows us to see the situation from a more objective point of view. It's almost like looking at the problem through someone else's eyes.

This shift in perspective can help us recognize patterns in our thinking and behavior that we may have overlooked and identify more effective strategies for dealing with the problem at hand. For example, if you're struggling with a difficult coworker, stepping back and speaking to yourself in the third person might help you recognize patterns in their behavior that you hadn't noticed before. You might also be able to identify specific triggers that cause you to react emotionally and develop a plan for responding more calmly and efficiently in the future.

Self-distancing can also be helpful in managing our emotions. By creating a sense of distance from our feelings, we can view them more objectively and identify healthier ways of coping. For example, if you're feeling overwhelmed and stressed, speaking to yourself in the third person might help you recognize the root causes of your stress and develop a plan for managing it more effectively.

Moreover, we often get stuck in our own heads when it comes to solving problems. It's like being in a maze with no clear exit, and the more we ruminate, the more we feel trapped. But what if I told you that you could escape this labyrinth by channeling your inner hero or mentor?

It sounds like a movie plot, but it's a real technique that can help you approach your problems with fresh eyes. Language might not seem like a big deal, but it can make a huge difference in how we perceive things. So, when you're faced with a difficult situation, think of someone you admire - whether it's a superhero like Wonder Woman or a wise mentor - and ask yourself how they would approach the problem.

By challenging yourself to view your challenges through the eyes of a compassionate outsider, you can cultivate a more objective and logical approach to problem-solving. By doing this, you create distance between yourself and the problem, allowing you to analyze it more objectively. For instance, you might say to yourself, "Take a breath, Wonder Woman, and analyze the situation calmly," or ask yourself, "Kevin, what advice do you think your mentor would have given you in this scenario?" This not only helps you think more rationally, but it also injects a sense of fun and creativity into the problem-solving process.

While it may seem like a simple concept, the practice of speaking kindly to yourself can have a profound effect on your mental well-being. But what if I told you that there's another way to silence that inner voice and achieve a sense of calm and peace?

Nature has long been touted as a powerful source of healing and rejuvenation for both the mind and body. By immersing yourself in the natural world, you can tap into its soothing and restorative properties, quieting your mind and fostering a sense of inner peace. Across various theoretical models and perspectives, a consensus has emerged that our relationship with nature plays an integral role in our well-being. One such model is the Attention Restoration Theory, which proposes that natural environments are particularly effective at capturing our involuntary attention, effortlessly engaging our minds in a way that promotes rest and relaxation.[8]

Furthermore, the biophilia hypothesis proposes that humans possess an inherent inclination to connect with and respond emotionally to the natural world.[9] By nurturing this biophilic tendency through involvement with nature, we can help alleviate existential anxieties and promote greater well-being.

The beauty and tranquility of nature have an undeniable influence on our overall well-being. Research has shown that being in contact with nature can enhance multiple aspects of our life.[10,11,12] For instance, it can elevate our life satisfaction and contribute to a more positive effect. In addition, it can help us find meaning in life and lead to feelings of elevation and vitality. Moreover, spending time in nature can enhance both our psychological and social well-being. In a world where technology has taken over, it's important to remember the benefits that nature can bring to our lives.

It's no secret that nature has a profound impact on our mood and well-being. Studies have shown that even after taking into account factors such as meteorological conditions, time of day, activity, camaraderie, and location type, and weekday, people experience greater levels of happiness in a natural setting than in an artificial environment.[13] Perhaps it's the fresh air, the sounds of birds chirping, the beauty of a sunset, or simply the feeling of being disconnected from the hustle and bustle of daily life that makes us feel so much better. Being surrounded by trees, flowers, and natural bodies of water can have a calming effect on our minds and bodies, reducing stress and anxiety levels.

It's no wonder that more and more people are taking up activities such as hiking, camping, and nature walks as a way to escape the pressures of modern life. It's a reminder that we are part of something much bigger than ourselves and that the natural world around us has a beauty and power that can make us feel more alive and connected.

In short, while speaking kindly to yourself can certainly help quiet that inner chatter, there's another powerful tool at your disposal: the restorative power of nature. So, if you feel your mind is stuck in a fruitless psychological loop, why not experiment and go to your nearest green space for a walk or just sit on the bench, inhale the fresh air beside a tree, and contemplate how someone else might deal with the problem or challenge you are facing?

External Chatter

Internal chatter is not the only noise that occupies the best of our brains. The external chatter is what leaves a deep impact too.

Silence is golden. Think about the quietest place you can go to. As per the information by the Guinness Book of World Records, the most silent place on planet Earth is in the building of Microsoft's Redmond, Washington, campus called an anechoic chamber. Microsoft has built a room wrapped in concrete and steel, sleeping over a divan of vibration-damping springs. In the room, fiberglass wedges protrude from the walls, ground, and ceiling, absorbing even the slightest sound. If you would google it, the photographs will give you a nightmarish look. Microsoft uses the room for different purposes, such as to test how loud a component, like the clicker of a mouse, really is. The quietness of the room is factually at a level out of human insight.

Sitting in a room so soundless might appear to be sometimes appealing, but some people are so unfamiliar with such levels of silence that, in a few minutes inside the chamber, they turn out to be disoriented. The room's principal designer, Hundraj Gopal, claims that some people find the room "deafening" and that it brings "a sense of fullness in the ears." You can hear the intolerable noise of your heartbeat, your sniff, and your stomach roiling. And most of all, you become too conscious of your own thoughts, your physique, and the time creeping by.

Despite the overwhelming silence of the soundproof room, our minds can still be plagued by external noise and chatter. For example, it may be of a person who commented on you on the street or your boss who randomly criticized your working style. It is essential to understand here that some noises are internal such as your self-talk, while other distractions or noise occur externally, such as negative remarks or deeds by other people, taunts, negative press, social media comments, etc. Critics or critical people are noise. They are not in the arena of life. People talking about you are just critical. The noise that comes due to these factors is vital to deal with, and how you deal with noise will directly affect your performance. Realize that external noise is only noise and is focused on distracting you from concentrating at the moment, particularly when situations are demanding. Nevertheless, you can select to turn down external noise or acquiesce to the pessimism of others.

When you do the former, that external noise gives birth to the internal noise. To put it the other way, internalizing outside negativity disturbs your thought patterns, generates doubts, and makes you question your aptitude for performing and accomplishing the things you seek in life.

For instance, admitting a negative comment as true from your friends before a competition might form doubts in your mind and heart about your capability to perform under pressure, or overhearing your teammates saying, "He must not be part of the starting line-up," can form mental strain and low energy levels, or your boss yelling at you for a mistake in the file make you procrastinate while working, or a mean argument with your sibling might lead to rage and distress, causing you to make atypical blunders. When we compare ourselves with others and doubt our abilities, we always end up regretting what we are not instead of allowing ourselves to enjoy who we are. But doing our best and attaining perfection is hardly ever the same. When perfection turns out to be the goal, it becomes the foe of development—and thus, it often diverts us from taking the crucial menace of progressing in life.

Moreover, the digital era has played a significant role in amplifying this external noise. Computers and mobile phones are part of life and are present at every step of our daily lives.[14] Social media and networking websites such as Snapchat, Instagram, YouTube, and TikTok broadcast bits of data about every member of our progressively huge and miscellaneous online networks. Often hollow in isolation, these moments we spend on the internet can easily be perceived as arbitrary noise and clutter.

Kenneth Gergen, the social psychologist, penned a book in 1991 called *The Saturated Self.* In the book, he cautioned of an Orwellian world where technology would 'saturate' humans to the extent of 'multiphrenia,' a disjointed form of the self that is pulled in several directions, and the person would be mislaid. As he said, "I am linked. Therefore I am."[15] I am sure Gergen would not have thought that his prediction would turn out to be so spot-on.

This is due to the fact that as our society exists more than 30 years later with its laptops, cell phones, and state-of-the-art electronic gadgets - seduced by the trap of the faded golden screen glow - we have never been more connected, more allied, and more assured to a virtual reality that numerous of us cannot imagine living without. Social comparison, jealousy, envy, and glamour are all we see throughout our day while scrolling the feed of Instagram, contributing to increasing this external noise such as social media news feeds, notifications, emails, text messages, etc. You might now question, *So, Trent, how can we get rid of these external noises?* The answer is simple. You can deal with your life's external noise by filtering the destructive comments you hear and paying more heed to constructive feedback. When we selectively digest information, we can stay more attentive.

One more way of dealing with negativity and tuning down this external noise is refocusing on the things that are important. When you notice the external noise is there, interject those thoughts with a statement like, "It's nothing, just a noise trying to distract me." Instantly following that signal, stipulate what you want to hang on to, and say, "Now, focus on...." Remember, what you choose to divert your attention to is a matter of choice, *so choose wisely.*

Chapter 6: Acting

Opposite

"Embrace the paradox of resilience, where the greatest strength lies in moments of vulnerability, and the path to triumph emerges by embracing the unlikeliest of choices."

Have you ever felt fumes coming out of your ears so loud from anger you could hardly breathe? Or have you ever felt so frustrated you wanted to burst out on the first person who comes across you? For instance, you might have called your internet service provider, and they kept you on hold for an hour. You waited patiently for the first few minutes, but as time passed, your patience grew thinner, thinking, *do they think I have got the entire day for them?* The moment the customer representative connects on the phone again, you feel the extreme emotional urge to lash out.

But stop…you didn't do that. You decided to control your urge, save your energy, take a step back, and calmly connect with the technician since you have been practicing the 'opposite action' techniques! So now, instead of saying things that you might have regretted later, you got your problem solved. And that, ladies and gentlemen, is what 'acting opposite' is all about!

Are We Dictated by Our Emotions?

Well, technically, yes, we definitely are dictated by our emotions. Some things occur in life that are totally opposite of what we expected. Inevitabilities create stressful thoughts and, in return, create stressful emotions like guilt, shame, depression, sadness, anger, and fear. What's more, these emotions take the wheel of our life. In turn, they trigger emotions inside that we feel, at times, unable to control, and quite often than not, we let those emotions take the best of us.

I am sure you must have seen individuals in your life who become irritated, gloomy, or dreadful and let those emotions to take-over the rational part of their brains, which, in turn, shows that they then reach conclusions and make decisions with possibly life-altering consequences. We, as humans, possess the power to decide if we want to act on our instincts or not. We might, at some point, become so accustomed to acting instinctively that we judge that's how we are when in reality, habits and behaviors are changeable because, at the end of the day, that's what makes us human.

There are situations in our lives that are inevitable. However, we always have the power to alter our life situations and fight back stronger. When you decide that you're going to get ahead in life, you choose to give yourself the power to decide the best decision for yourself. You choose to live self-assuredly by determining first where you're going and then evaluating the steps to get there. As

James Russell Lowell said, *"Such power there is in clear-eyed self-restraint."* There surely is. When you would decide that you want to gain control over your own life and take ownership of your own actions and decisions, things can only get better from there. Taking control back from the negative thoughts and the following adverse behaviors is undoubtedly not a pleasant or easy experience, but developing the confidence, skills, and resources necessary to assert yourself in the face of adversity and to make choices that align with your values and goals is what really matters.

As a matter of fact, emotions are really meant to be running all day long in us because that's what they really are – 'e-motions.' We can also regard them as children who we can't let drive the car but, on the other hand, can't lock them in a trunk either.

Inevitabilities have so many emotions intertwined. For example, the death of a loved one can cause you to feel anger for them for leaving you alone in the world, for the things left unsaid, or for being taken too soon. You might also feel guilt inside your heart if the last conversation you had with your deceased loved one was terrible or if you did not say or get a chance to say goodbye or I love you. Moreover, you might feel fear in this type of situation that you might be taken or another loved one will be taken or fear that you will never get over this.

All these sentiments come with behavioral urges that direct us to act in specific ways. From time to time, we employ negative coping skills to get rid of tender emotions since it seems like it's the easiest or the only way to deal with them. For instance, when dreaded, we frequently feel the impulse to dodge or escape a circumstance. When annoyed, we swiftly turn out to be defensive or react aggressively. When miserable or dejected, we have the tendency to pull out, isolate, and become inactive. With embarrassment and the feeling of culpability, we characteristically hide, dodge, or apologize to others.

Emotions are essential due to the fact that they offer us information and signals regarding things to pay heed to in our day-to-day lives. Sometimes, a sentiment 'fits the facts of a situation' and encourages us in the direction of effective action. For example, feeling nervous about an upcoming project could be your motivator to prepare as much as possible. However, there may be a time when an emotion 'does not fit the facts of the circumstance,' and acting on an emotional urge is ineffective. For instance, feeling extreme anxiety regarding eating dinner at a cafe does not 'fit the facts of the circumstance' and might cause you to feel the urge to side-step socializing and going out for dinner at all.

As time passes, this avoidance behavior only turns out to make the anxiety worse. Furthermore, it could start to influence your relationships negatively.

In this instance, you might want to observe that you are undergoing the impulse to dodge eating out and take an 'opposite action,' which aligns more with your living standards. For example, pushing yourself a little to go out and have meals at a small local restaurant with fewer people (despite feeling afraid) would be all about taking the opposite action.

Another example could be that you might have been working on a project with a co-worker, and you've put a lot of effort and time into it. However, when you present it to your boss, they are unimpressed and provide negative feedback. Your first instinct might be to defend your work and argue with your boss. But reacting defensively could escalate the situation and damage your relationship with your boss. Instead, in this situation, you might want to sort the situation out calmly and logically to defend your position. You can listen to your boss's feedback and ask questions to understand their perspective. Then, calmly explain your thought process and suggest alternative solutions that align with their feedback. This approach shows that you are open to feedback, willing to collaborate, and capable of finding creative solutions.

Now, you might question, *but Trent, I don't really understand the need for acting opposite to my emotions in the first place.* Well, while your feelings might be valid, the behaviors that these emotional urges cause may injure your relationships, preventing you from achieving imperative things in your life. Moreover, retorting to a tender emotional state in the same unaccommodating ways doesn't make you feel it. Also, acting on emotionally charged urges might strengthen rather than lessen your emotions. As I said earlier, your feelings just become stronger and make you feel worse eventually.

We often resort to the same actions to feel better when we experience negative emotions repeatedly. We tend to respond to stress the same way again and again, even if it is not effective, because we are reinforced by the perceived emotions of feeling better. For instance, you might have gone to a sports event with a friend and experienced high anxiety. You ultimately decided to flee the arena and go home. While at home, you self-soothe by scrolling through social media only to feel better. So, what will you do next time? Ultimately, your urge to act on the emotion and then leave the event reinforces your uncomfortableness even more. This could be because you now, even more, feel how the home is your safe zone and how comfortable you are staying within the four walls.

However, ultimately the goal is to learn how to feel comfortable while feeling uncomfortable. Now, this might sound a little strange to you, but it is a central concept in personal growth and self-improvement. Many of us have a natural tendency to avoid uncomfortable situations or emotions, but this can actually limit our ability to grow and change. By learning to be comfortable with discomfort, we open ourselves up to new experiences and opportunities, and we become better equipped to handle the challenges that life throws our way.

And how do I do it, Trent? You might ask. Well, just like the example I gave you about fleeing the sports event, expose yourself to new and challenging situations. This might involve setting small, achievable goals that push you outside of your comfort zone. As you achieve these goals, you'll build confidence and resilience, and you'll be better able to handle increasingly difficult tasks. Similarly, practice mindfulness and acceptance by paying attention to the present moment in a non-judgmental way. By focusing on the present and accepting whatever emotions or sensations you're feeling, you can develop a sense of calm and equanimity in the face of discomfort.

And this is also where opposite action skills come in. Practicing the opposite reaction boosts us to act in a new manner instead of depending on the typical comeback. It is important to remember that we should only choose to act opposite to an urge if acting opposite would bear positive or fruitful results. This relates to instincts associated with negative feelings only, as working on urges associated with positive emotions is not typically challenging.

But What is Acting Opposite Skill?

It often happens that we become inclined to act on our instincts and urges because they seem to be the absolute right thing to do at the moment. Sensibly, nevertheless, we can understand that acting out of urges is not always in our best interest. For example, imagine that you had a frustrating day at work and then came home in a bad mood. If you then proceed to lash out at your partner or family members, you may feel a temporary release of your anger. However, because your outburst was fuelled by the initial emotional response, it can cause more conflicts, and the anger is likely to linger and continue to cause you distress.

On the other hand, if you had instead taken some time to process your feelings and reflect on what might have caused your frustration, you might have had a better understanding of the source of your anger, and you would have been able to address it more effectively. Moreover, since acting in this manner is likely mostly unrelated to people's standards and morals, doing so can activate secondary adverse effects, such as guilt or self-effacement. 'Acting opposite' to passionately charged impulses is recommended to fight this problem.

In this case, by not acting on your instant emotional urges and instead taking a step back to reflect and process your feelings, you may diminish the intensity of your anger and find more constructive ways to cope with it. It's important to learn to pause and reflect before acting on our emotional impulses. This can be difficult to do, especially when emotions are running high, but with practice, it can become a habit.

In 'Dialectical Behavioral Therapy' (DBT), people are trained with the 'acting opposite' skills to their desires to diminish the intensity of the related delicate sentiment. For instance, instead of physically hurting someone out of anger, you might want to remove yourself from the scene or retort to the situation in a more civil style instead of making the situation worse. A lot of research studies have revealed that DBT is helpful in treating impulsive behavior.[16,17] When you learn the opposite acting skill, you become capable of controlling maladaptive characteristic responses and imitating an adaptive response. Quite obviously, you need to practice the skill to see the outcome.

Certainly, as a human being, you possess emotion, but that doesn't mean you always have to act according to those feelings. By acquiring knowledge of and practicing 'acting opposite' skills, you'll have a better chance of deciding whether or not to follow your urges and whether those urges are leading you toward the right actions. Think about it for a moment; we all have sentiments that can make us do things we would rather not prefer to do because, at the moment, our feelings prevail over the rational part of our minds. In a nutshell, a specific sentiment directs the show, influencing us to take a specific course of action. Nevertheless, rather than acting on those sentiments, we can employ the opposite action in its place and save ourselves from regretting our choices later.

For instance, let's consider that you have been feeling miserable since you broke up with your partner. Your emotions tell you to cut yourself from the world, stay at home, and self-isolate since everything out there would remind you about your past relationship with your ex. So, if your feeling (sadness) is manipulating you to stay caged at home, the 'opposite action' skill will help you to do something different. In case of sadness or when we're feeling gloomy, we might not gauge what's wrong or what to do instead.

For example, when feeling down, it's common to want to escape the constant stream of disruptive thoughts and regain a sense of mental tranquility. However, instead of succumbing to self-pity and negative self-talk, you can shift your focus toward the positive aspects of your life. This can be achieved through practices such as gratitude journaling, meditation, or performing a random act of kindness. It's not necessary to start with grand gestures; even small, everyday things can be appreciated by changing your perspective and gaining a deeper understanding of your emotional system and the resulting behaviors. This shift in focus can help redirect your thoughts towards a more positive outlook.

Now you might ask, *Trent, are you asking me to just ignore my feelings?* Absolutely not. In fact, what's important about opposite action is identifying that you are experiencing a particular emotion in the first place.

Having that elementary emotional knowledge is critical for being capable of executing opposite actions. Nevertheless, this doesn't imply that you should thrust, overlook or disregard the emotion. It's more about simply acknowledging it, which generates a detachment and separation between your emotions and your behaviors.

Can You Learn Opposite Action?

Have you heard Newton's Third Law, *"For every action, there is an equal and opposite reaction?"* Relax, I am not going to test your Physics knowledge or talk about rocket science. Instead, we are actually talking about using the opposite actions and coping techniques to turn that scowl into a U-shaped smile. Opposite action can be employed with sentiments that are either baseless or unfounded in their degree of intensity. To put it the other way, you can employ this method when you are confronted with uninvited sentiments that are not defensible no matter what. These sentiments are usually tied with action impulses that are destructive or on the damaging side, so using opposite actions allows you to swap these unaccommodating behaviors with more constructive and accommodating ones.

For instance, a person may have a tendency to overeat when he or she is feeling stressed or anxious. This is a negative behavior that can have negative consequences on the person's health and well-being in the long term. One way to counter and act opposite to these urges could be to give a name to the uninvited sentiment (overeating in this case) as a way of better understanding and managing that urge. By giving the emotional urge a name, you can more easily identify and acknowledge when the sentiment is present, which can help you to take steps to address those emotional urges and act opposite to them. For example, the person could name his or her overeating urge as an 'invader' since it intrudes on his habit of eating healthy, which is unwanted and uninvited.

So, let me put forward some techniques in front of you that might assist you in contesting inevitabilities as well as the feelings that arise from them. This is how we will build tolerance and charge forward. These procedures will help in practicing opposite actions to counter our impulsive emotional urges, as they may not lead to positive outcomes for us. Essentially, the whole point is to consciously act opposite to your emotional urge. If your actions are doing more damage than good, try behaving the opposite. Some of the opposite actions that you can employ to common urges are discussed below:

1. Fear:

If you feel frightened, approach the inducement that triggers anxiety. Try to face your fear and do things to grow your sense of management, control and form control over your distress. To face your fear, you can utilize exposure techniques. This involves gradually exposing yourself to the source of your fear in a controlled manner, allowing you to become more comfortable and desensitized over time. But that's not all. To cultivate that sweet sense of management and control, you can engage in activities such as setting goals, developing problem-solving skills, and practicing self-care. These actions empower you to take charge of your circumstances and build resilience in the face of hardships.

Now, let's talk about the antithesis of fear—courage! Activities that promote acting opposite to fear involve stepping outside of your comfort zone, taking calculated risks, and embracing new experiences. It can be trying that daring adventure sport you've always dreamed of, speaking your mind on a public stage, or fearlessly engaging strangers in conversation. By actively engaging in these activities, you can develop a sense of courage and expand your comfort zone. Remember, each person's journey is unique, so it's important to explore different strategies and find what works best for you in facing fears and developing a sense of control.

Fear can manifest in many different ways and can be triggered by a variety of things. You can feel the fear of failure, fear of rejection, or fear of the unknown. Remember that by engaging in the fear, you prove to yourself that the fear is an unreliable master, which will give you the courage to confront it time and time again.

Engaging with fear and facing it directly can help to demonstrate to ourselves that our fears are not as powerful as we may have thought. By taking action in the face of fear, we can show ourselves that we are capable of handling the situation and that we can cope with the negative outcomes that we may have feared. This process of facing our fears can help to decrease the power and influence that fear has over us and can lead to greater feelings of confidence and courage.

Additionally, by engaging with our fears and understanding them more fully, we can also gain insight into the underlying thoughts, beliefs, and assumptions that drive them, and by examining and challenging them, we can change them to be more rational, realistic, and less extreme. This can help us to see that fear is often based on an unreliable or distorted perspective and that our anxiety is not necessarily an accurate indicator of reality.

Furthermore, by confronting the fear repeatedly over time, you are numbing yourself to it, making it less powerful over time. This can allow you to build up a sense of mastery and control over your fears, making it less likely that they will overwhelm you in the future. It's important to note that this process takes time, effort, and patience, but with persistence and the right approach, anyone can learn to confront their fears and live a more fulfilling life.

2. Sadness:

If you feel gloomy, approach, don't circumvent the circumstances you're distressed with. Just like confronting your fear, try to master your feeling. Don't coop up within yourself – pray, get out, and keep yourself moving!

Note that keeping busy does not imply not acknowledging your feelings but facing them and moving on. Engaging with sadness does not mean dwelling on it or becoming overwhelmed by it. It's important to balance processing the sadness with self-care and engagement in activities that bring joy and fulfillment.

Similarly, to fear, by engaging with sadness repeatedly over time, you will be able to see it as a normal and natural emotion that comes and goes and that it is not as powerful as it may have seemed before. It can help to reduce the power and influence that sadness has over you and lead to greater feelings of well-being and resilience. For instance, someone is going through a difficult situation, such as the loss of a loved one. They are feeling a deep sense of sadness and grief. They may find themselves isolating from friends and family, avoiding activities that they used to enjoy, and feeling a lack of energy or motivation. In this type of situation, the person might avoid going outside and stay in their room all day. However, the opposite action to it would be that instead of staying inside the dark shadows, the person could try going for a walk or doing some light exercise. Going out into nature, being with friends and family, and giving your mind some space in the surrounding definitely helps to increase energy levels and improve mood. As we develop tolerance through the grief process, we could even join a support group.

Spending time with your loved ones and participating in social activities can have a positive impact on mental well-being and can help to alleviate feelings of sadness. Having a strong support system can provide emotional support and a sense of belonging, which can be beneficial for individuals experiencing sadness or other mental health concerns.

I understand that you might feel flooded with different emotions and prefer to stay alone, but that only intensifies the feeling of loneliness and increases your sadness level. Prioritize spending time with your loved ones, as the power of love, care, and a kind word is often underestimated. Their support can be invaluable in strengthening your resilience and mental fortitude.

3. Guilt:

If your guilt is real and justified, i.e., if it fits the facts, then face it. Here by 'face it,' I mean that you need to experience the guilt. Apologize to others or yourself and try your best to mend the thoughts or behaviors encompassing the guilt. It can be helpful to reflect on the situation and understand the reasons for your actions, and then take full responsibility for them. If your actions have caused harm to others, it is important to make a sincere apology and take steps to repair the relationship. If the guilt is stemming from something you did to yourself, it may be helpful to practice self-compassion and forgiveness.

If your guilt does NOT fit the facts and is unjustified, then don't apologize or try to make up for it. Remember that in the start, you might just feel a little guilty about something, and then with time, it could start to take the best of you, going from mild feelings of remorse to debilitating feelings of shame and self-loathing. Moreover, when guilt is intense or prolonged, it can lead to negative consequences such as depression, anxiety, and stress. Moreover, when we allow guilt to control our thoughts and actions, it prevents us from taking steps to correct our mistakes and make amends, which can prolong the healing process and make the guilt worse.

By doing the opposite action to your feeling of guilt, you will be able to take steps to reduce the intensity of the emotion and move forward in a constructive way. This can include taking action to make amends, learning from your mistakes, and using the experience to make positive changes in the future. It's important to remember that applying the opposite action skill to guilt doesn't mean ignoring or dismissing the guilt; it's acknowledging it and taking appropriate actions. This can help to reduce the intensity of the guilt, learn from the experience, and make amends to prevent similar situations in the future.

Let's say you have had a history of bullying peers and coworkers. You feel guilty for your actions and the harm caused to others. Now the first step toward applying the opposite acting skill would be to acknowledge and accept the guilt you feel for your actions rather than trying to suppress or ignore it. Then, you can proceed to exhibit kindness towards your colleagues both in the workplace and in various spheres of life. By actively demonstrating empathy towards others, you have the opportunity to make amends for your past behaviors and foster a deeper connection with your fellow human beings...

Along with all this, it is also important that you also engage in self-care activities and practice self-compassion in how you want to move forward. Making compensations to others and yourself, acknowledging your mistakes, and actively working to make things right are vital steps.

4. Anger:

When you get mad, try not to act out of anger at that moment and distance yourself. This means refraining from physically retaliating or responding with hurtful words when someone makes you furious, and instead choosing to side-step the situation or avoid that person. Try to understand or empathize with the opposite party, striving to grasp the 'nugget of truth.' It's crucial that you pay attention and show sympathy, even if it's to a lesser extent. For instance, if you find yourself used up by tenacious or devastating anger, make a choice to apply the opposite action to dowse the igniting fire of anger. You can choose to foster an attitude of calmness and acceptance. Take a few deep breaths and let yourself become peaceful into acceptance of what is. You can vigorously decrease your state of hyper-arousal by taking a few deep breaths, indulging in self-soothing, and thinking optimistically about others. Instead of shielding yourself in the spikey wires of denial, pick to open yourself up to the authenticity of your experience—gratitude!

5. Shame:

Shame is a relentless specter, lurking in the shadows of our minds, haunting our thoughts, and leaving an indelible mark on our souls. It whispers cruel judgments, amplifies our insecurities, and erodes our self-worth. Like an invisible weight upon our shoulders, it saps our joy, stifles our growth, and undermines our confidence like an emotional abyss engulfing us and isolating us in a world of self-doubt and self-blame, eventually dictating our actions, and casting a dark cloud over our mental and physical well-being. Some individuals may feel strong shame related to a particular event or situation, while others experience a more general and hard-to-identify sense of shame. The intensity of shame can change depending on your own self-esteem, your past experiences, and the culture you live in. For instance, let's say you are being subjected to frequent criticism, comparison, or disapproval and have started to feel self-conscious about your abilities. As a result, you begin to believe this narrative and experience shame. Instead of dwelling on negative thoughts and self-talk, try to reframe those thoughts.

There exists a powerful force that can shatter the hold

of shame and set us free: the invigorating embrace of pride! When we embrace our accomplishments, honor our true selves, and bask in the glow of self-acceptance, shame's power weakens. For example, instead of succumbing to thoughts like, *"I'm so ashamed of my mistakes, I'm a failure,"* you can shift your perspective and remind yourself, *"I accept that I have some imperfections, but they don't define me. I am capable of growth and learning from my experiences, and I deserve self-compassion and a chance to thrive."*

This shift from shame to self-compassion highlights the transformative power of embracing one's humanity and worthiness, fostering a mindset of acceptance and personal growth. To act counter to these thoughts, celebrate progress and victories from within yourself. You can love yourself while accepting the past. Likewise, it is also imperative to excuse yourself and move on if the shame is something that fits the fact.

It is not healthy to suppress or deny feelings of shame. It is important to acknowledge and process these feelings in a healthy way. Holding back from facing others can make the situation worse and prolong the healing process. It is important to remember that everyone makes mistakes, and it is possible to learn from them and grow as a person. Instead of trying to suppress or deny feelings of shame, it can be helpful to talk to a trusted friend or professional counselor to work through these feelings and gain a better understanding of what led to the situation.

We are all humans, and we all make mistakes. But does that mean we don't give ourselves any leverage? We're stronger when we accept our mistakes and move on in the direction to become better, unafraid to face anyone. That's better than being rigid on the slipups one makes and refusing to accept them!

To summarize these techniques for you, I have formed a table for a clearer understanding.

Incidents That Might Trigger an Emotional Urge Within You	The Urge That You Might Feel	Usual Responses in Such Types of Incidents	The Opposite Action You Could Try
Arguing	Anger	You might feel agitated to hit or attack verbally or physically.	You can remain silent and/or show concern and/or walk away.
Making a mistake	Shame	You might have demeaning thoughts about yourself. As a result, you try to escape to hide or isolate yourself.	You can accept the mistake and be confident. Nobody is perfect. Working is a process.
Giving a presentation	Fear	Being anxious before the meeting and feeling fear of making a mistake	Challenge your negative thoughts by questioning their validity or practicing public speaking, learning about the audience, and preparing a solid and organized presentation.
Losing	Sadness	You might avoid contact with people, become inactive, and overthink the loss.	Go out, interact with people, and accept the loss. Be proud that you are in the arena trying your best. Keep Moving!
Unable to spend time with your family	Guilt	You might ruminate on the situation and degrade yourself.	Apologize to the family and yourself, and make changes to the routine a bit that would allow more time with your family.

Remember that the opposite action will work finest when your sentiments 'do NOT fit the facts' of an existing state of affairs. This means that your feelings, strength, and their extent, are NOT CONSTRUCTIVE in assisting you to attain your objectives. It is likewise imperative to go all in with the skill. Involve in opposite behaviors and employ opposite sentimental statements, thinking patterns, facial expressions, voice pitch, and body postures! The whole point of the conversation is to realize that engaging in opposite behaviors is a key component of using the opposite action skill to reduce intense or uninvited emotions. By engaging in behaviors that are opposite to the emotion, you can begin to disrupt the pattern of the emotion and reduce its intensity.

For instance, if you are feeling anxious, counteract with sentimental statements and do the opposite action, you might repeat the phrase *"I am calm and in control"* to offset the anxious thoughts and feelings. Similarly, to reinforce opposite thinking patterns if you are feeling down, you might focus on finding three things you are grateful for to shift from negative thoughts to positive thoughts. Likewise, for opposite voice pitch and body postures, if you are feeling anxious, you might speak in a lower, slower, and more measured tone to counteract the high-pitched, fast-paced speech that may be associated with anxiety and practice open, relaxed, and upright body postures to counteract the closed, tense, and hunched body postures that may be associated with anxiety.

If you heard about this technique for the first time and are new to practicing it, start with less intense feelings first. Start by recognizing your feelings and the behaviors' urge linked with those feelings. Then, question yourself if your feelings fit the fact of the situation and if behaving according to that emotion would be effective. Once you get the answer, question yourself again, *Do I want to change my emotion?* Then comprehend what would be the opposite action and do exactly that. In the end, repeat doing so until the feeling declines enough. Once you have become skilled at this procedure, set off to more intense and challenging feelings so you can better deal with your sentiments!

Now, to bring this idea into practice, keep connected to this chapter for the next two-three days or for as long as you need. Evaluate your day-to-day actions, behaviors, emotional urges, and your responses. I have designed a small practice table for you so that you can be mindful of your urges and the responses and then fill it out accordingly.

Incident That Triggered the Emotional Urge Within Me	The Urge That I Felt (Sadness, Depression, Fear, Anger, Guilt, Disgust, Shame, Frustration, Etc)	My Usual Response in Such Type of Incidents	The Opposite Action I Tried in Its Place

Think about a young man learning to cook. Do you think it's an easy process? Well, not really. It's a long and challenging one, as it requires a combination of technical skills, creativity, and experience. The cook knows nothing from the start and, with time, master's basic kitchen skills, such as knife skills, food safety, and kitchen sanitation. You would give that cook time and flexibility to prepare a variety of basic dishes first, including sauces, stocks, and soups. Along the way, as they gain experience, they will learn more advanced cooking techniques, such as sautéing, braising, and roasting.

As time passes, they will begin to develop their own style and techniques, learning to work with a wider variety of ingredients and to create new and innovative dishes. And who knows, one day, that young man who didn't have the skills to work with a knife properly would become skilled to manage a kitchen, lead his own team and manage resources effectively in his own restaurant.

The path to that chef becoming a master chef was not without difficulties. It took a lot of hard work, dedication, and sacrifice, and who knows how many times he would have thought to quit. The long hours, high stress, and the pressure to constantly create new and exciting dishes might have crippled the cook with strain.

But he would reach that position with constant effort, consistency, and hard work. Just as you may give time to a new cook learning cooking to prepare a perfect meal, by teaching them and letting them cook a simple meal that is not too complex, give yourself the same kind of leverage and act accordingly while practicing since practicing 'Opposite Action' and getting the results would not happen overnight. Like I always say, it's important to note that changing your behaviors can take time. You need to test yourself in slow, steady, and manageable steps. It's not how we begin the journey; it's how we finish it. Please remember that!

Chapter 7: Metabolizing Our Victories

Before you were born,
And were still too tiny for
The human eye to see,
You won the race for life
From among 250 million competitors.

And yet,
How fast you have forgotten
Your strength,
When your very existence
It is proof of your greatness.

You were born a winner,
A warrior,
One who defied the odds
By surviving the most gruesome
Battle of them all.

And now that you are a giant,
Why do you even doubt victory
Against smaller numbers,
And wider margins?
The only walls that exist,
Are those you have placed in your mind?

And whatever obstacles you conceive,
Exist only because you have forgotten
What you have already!

The beautiful words of the poetry above are painted by Suzy Kassem in her poem 'Remember Your Greatness' from her book *Rise Up and Salute the Sun*. If I talk about myself, I am left in awe of the complexity and depth of the vivid imagery she has painted through her work of art, reminding the readers of their own strengths and abilities. If you take a deeper insight into what she's implying through these simple yet profound words, you will realize she's talking about the odds that you overcame just when you were in the race to get born and survive. It's comprehendible that we should not doubt our abilities to overcome obstacles and achieve victory in our lives. The poem also implies that the only limitations that exist in our lives are the ones that we have put in our minds, and it encourages us to remember our own greatness and not let self-doubt hold us back. Such an empowering, motivational, and inspirational message to remember our own strength, potential, and greatness!

And why shouldn't we remember and be proud of it, after all? We, humans, have so many things to be delighted of, be grateful for, and relish in life. When we feel a sense of pride in our accomplishments and successes, and realize how we have achieved goals and overcome challenges over time, it can turn out to be a source of personal satisfaction and self-esteem for us. Furthermore, it can also serve as motivation to strive for further achievements. However, it is important to remember that pride can also be a double-edged sword. Excessive pride can lead to disregarding or belittling the contributions and perspectives of others, which can harm relationships and hinder personal growth. It may also prevent individuals from acknowledging their own mistakes or seeking help when needed, as they may feel invulnerable or superior. Overall, while a healthy amount of pride can be positive and motivating, excessive pride can indeed have detrimental effects.

So, finding a healthy balance and realizing our achievements not only helps us in apprehending our worth but also enables others to recognize their own value.

By understanding and embracing our capabilities and accomplishments, we create an environment where others can also recognize and appreciate their own strengths.

An Appetite for Victories

Have you ever heard someone say, *"Dude, I'm savoring my happiness!"* Well, in case you didn't, think about it for a moment and wonder what does it actually mean?

First of all, savoring means enjoying something to its full capacity, and when this concept is applied to the psychology of human beings, it takes us on a ride to a new perspective. It tells how savoring, when seen in a different light, is the act of deliberately paying attention to and enjoying positive experiences. Research has shown that savoring can increase happiness by helping us to focus on, and appreciate, positive experiences rather than letting them pass by unnoticed.[18] Savoring can also increase the intensity and duration of positive emotions and can even increase the likelihood of future positive experiences by creating positive memories. Additionally, it decreases stress and increases feelings of gratitude and social connectedness. Therefore, it is often recommended as a strategy for increasing overall well-being and happiness.

When you learn to savor a moment, you fully appreciate and relish in the good things that happen rather than letting them pass by unnoticed. Just like on a hike, where we often get caught up in savoring the big things we experience, like reaching the summit of a mountain or witnessing a breathtaking panoramic view, it's important to remember that the small things in life should also be appreciated. These little moments and details that often go unnoticed can be just as enjoyable, if not more so, than the big ones. For instance, while hiking, we might pause to admire the delicate flowers blooming alongside the trail or watch a roadrunner scurry across the desert trail of the Franklin Mountains in El Paso, Texas. We should make a conscious effort to slow down and savor the small things in life. A warm hug from a loved one, the taste of a well-made cup of tea, the feeling of a soft fleece blanket on a cold day

– these little things can bring us a great deal of joy. We can take a moment to appreciate the warmth of the sun on our skin, the taste of a delicious meal, or the sound of a loved one's laughter. These small things may seem insignificant in the grand scheme of things, but they can bring us joy and happiness in the present moment when we press pause and reflect.

By taking the time to appreciate the small things, we can find meaning and happiness in our lives, even during the most challenging times. Just as a hike can provide us with a sense of accomplishment, a renewed perspective, and a deeper connection to nature, taking the time to savor the small things in life can bring us a sense of contentment and fulfillment. We should not get too caught up in the destination but rather enjoy the journey and appreciate the small good things that happen along the way and build upon them.

Without learning to savor the positive experiences, our world stays somewhat vague, with experiences and emotions blending together without being fully experienced or appreciated. We may miss out on the joy and fulfillment that come with fully experiencing positive moments.

You can also describe savoring the moment as the set

of cognitive or behavioral strategies that individuals use to regulate the intensity or duration of positive feelings. These strategies can include things such as paying attention to and fully experiencing encouraging events, reflecting on experiences, expressing gratitude for constructive happenings, sharing uplifting experiences with others, and creating positive memories of the events. You can employ these strategies to enhance the positive feelings associated with you winning a game or getting the promotion and prolong the duration of these positive feelings. For example, when you win a baseball game or when you get a promotion at work.

The broaden-and-build theory of positive affect proposed by Barbara Fredrickson[19] explains that positive emotions broaden an individual's momentary thought-action repertoire, which in turn can build physical, intellectual, and social resources. Savoring positive experiences operates in line with this theory by helping individuals to broaden and build their positive affect. Thus, we can claim that savoring allows us to fully experience and appreciate positive events, which can increase the intensity and duration of positive emotions.

Additionally, savoring increases the likelihood of future positive experiences by creating positive memories, which can serve as personal resources, fostering the development of interpersonal resources. Moreover, it also encourages social connectedness and gratitude, further enhancing the development of interpersonal resources.

When we acknowledge our victories and breathe constructive experiences into our system, it cuts through the negatively aligned narratives from within ourselves and combats the self-destructive views that we sometimes impose on our beings. It's okay to make mistakes and not be at the top of our game all the time, and it's okay to celebrate small victories.

Let me give you the example of a farmer here who had a field filled with wheat. Every day, the farmer would wake up early and work tirelessly in the field, tending to his crops. However, he was plagued by thoughts of self-doubt, constantly dwelling on past mistakes and feeling like he would never have a successful harvest.

One day, a wise old sage visited the farmer and noticed his struggles. The sage told the farmer that in order to combat his thoughts, he needed to start acknowledging his victories, no matter how small they may seem. The farmer was skeptical but decided to give it a try. From that day forward, the farmer made a point to take note of every small victory in his field. He wrote down things like *"I removed the weeds from the field,"* *"I fertilized the soil,"* and *"I saw the first sprouts of wheat today."* At first, it felt strange to focus on such small achievements, but as he continued to do it, he began to notice a shift in his mindset.

He started to feel more positive about himself and his abilities. He began to see that he was capable of achieving things and that he had more to be proud of than he had previously realized. He started to focus on the present and the future rather than dwelling on the past. So, when harvest season came, the farmer was amazed to see that his field was filled with a bountiful crop of wheat. He realized that by acknowledging his small victories and focusing on the positive, he was able to combat his negative thoughts and self-doubt and had a successful harvest because of it.

What do you think that means? Well, that means that by acknowledging our victories, no matter how small they may seem, we can combat bad feelings and self-doubt and ultimately achieve our goals. Always remember that registering our victories not only prolongs the feeling but also can be used to reframe negative thoughts or core beliefs. This gives us ammunition because it proves to us that we do have things to be proud of. It builds confidence in us which, in turn, can help us lean into the cause and develop more tolerance.

For instance, in Chapter 3, we shared the common thought that many of us might have, like "I don't have what it takes." In actual fact, you do have it, but you just need to realize it. By completing a project at work or by simply saying 'hi' to a colleague, you accomplished a certain part of the day that you should feel proud about. When we make it a habit to acknowledge our victories, big or small, our focus doesn't remain stuck on the outcome but rather that we went for it, and that in itself is a victory.

I went to the party...

I talked to a peer at lunch...

I sent a difficult email...

I did not second-guess myself...

All the above are examples of what small victories look like that eventually take us on the road to achieving our big goals. Cherish these small victories, and even if you fail, you will have in hand the experiences and things you succeeded in doing, along the way. Victories, be they big or small, don't have to be a total success. Just the fact that you went for it is the main part! Try acknowledging them and then ask yourself, *'Yes, buddy, now how did that feel, huh?'*

Taking the Time

Taking the time to reflect on our accomplishments and feeling proud of ourselves for achieving them can create power within each of our own stories. By taking the time to reflect on your achievements, you can gain a sense of perspective and recognize that you have accomplished more than you may have realized, just like the farmer did.

Taking the time involves just that—Take the time for yourself! We often lead busy lives, and in the rush of things, it's easy to forget to take a step back and appreciate ourselves. That's where the concept of 'taking the time' comes in. It's about giving yourself permission to pause, reflect, and celebrate your accomplishments.

Taking the time for yourself can manifest in various forms. One way is to take stock of your accomplishments by writing them down. It might sound simple, but this practice can be incredibly powerful.

By seeing your achievements in black and white, you're not only acknowledging them, but you're also reminding yourself of your capabilities and strengths. Another way is to give yourself positive affirmations. These are statements that reaffirm your positive qualities and can help boost your self-confidence.

Saying things like *"I am capable and strong"* or *"I am worthy of love and success"* might feel a little cheesy at first, but over time, they can become powerful tools for self-affirmation and empowerment.

Moreover, you can acknowledge your success or simply any little growth or achievement through celebratory and enjoyable actions, for instance, when professional soccer players celebrate a goal by sliding on the grass, hugging each other, and running around the pitch or when baseball players high-five each other, jumping up and down at the home plate after hitting a game-winning home run or throwing their gloves or hats in the air to celebrate winning the World Series. These all are examples of savoring the moment. It's a way of acknowledging their hard work and basking in the glow of their accomplishment. This makes sense because we need to take the time and acknowledge our hard work—It must not go unnoticed!

We can apply this same principle to our own lives, regardless of whether we're professional athletes or not. Taking the time to celebrate our successes - whether it's a promotion at work, completing a challenging project, or achieving a personal goal - can be a form of savoring. By doing so, we're allowing ourselves to fully appreciate our hard work and savor the positive emotions that come with it.

It is suggested that savoring is a process through which good feeling increases consciousness, promotes exploration, and strengthens behavioral abilities.[20] Research has even revealed that every day present-moment savoring can direct us to significant improvements in happiness levels.[21] Just by taking a few minutes each day to focus on something positive in your life, such as a beautiful sunset, a delicious meal, or a moment of connection with a loved one, you can notice a significant change in your mindset and how you perceive things and the positive stuff in your life.

One study suggests that deliberately meditating on ideas and feelings associated with a good event for 15 minutes each day for three days can improve wellness and happiness.[22] Another study published in the *Journal of Mental Health* suggested that using positive imagery or memorabilia to reminiscence positive memories over the course of two sessions of ten minutes each per day for a week, showed an increase in positive affect.[23] Furthermore, employing diverse present-moment savoring exercises every day, one week for each exercise, and engaging for a few minutes in the experience can increase contentment after one week of settling the intervention.[24]

It is important to note here that savoring is not just about feeling good at the moment, but it also creates a lasting impact on overall well-being and life satisfaction.

Let's Practice Savoring the Moment

Before reading this page any further, make sure you are in a comfortable position. If you have a coffee mug in your hand right now, put it on the side table.

Now that I have your complete attention, let's do a brief savoring-the-moment exercise.

1. Take a few minutes to sit in a comfortable and quiet place. Close your eyes and take a deep breath in through your nose and out through your mouth.

2. Think about something that you currently achieved or any small or big growth in life you made, be it personal or professional. For example, you may focus on how you mustered up the courage to engage in a difficult conversation and how it all went alright. You can also think about the time you won a baseball game or how you helped a person (that counts because being empathetic is a personal achievement).

3. Try to pay attention to the sensation, emotion, or thought as deeply as possible. Try to notice the different aspects of the experience, such as the background of that time

and the feelings, or recall how you felt with the positive thing you felt or what happened to you during the day. Allow yourself to fully immerse yourself in that moment.

4. Once done, take a few more deep breaths, and try to express gratitude for the experience. It could be in the form of a small gratitude note or a verbal expression telling yourself out loud how you felt.

5. Repeat this exercise as often as you can throughout the day, focusing on different sensations, emotions, or thoughts each time.

6. Take a moment to reflect on how the exercise made you feel. How did it change your perception of the present moment?

7. Repeat the exercise regularly and note down any changes in your perception of the present moment and overall well-being.

It is important to remember that savoring the present moment is a skill that takes time and practice to develop, so be patient with yourself, and don't get discouraged if you find it difficult at first. For your practice, a worksheet is given below for you to note down your experience at different times of the day.

Time of the Day	The Place I am Sitting At	The Positive Event I am Savoring	The Emotions I Feel After Savoring It
			(Enlightenment, Contentment, Peaceful, Gratitude, Satisfaction, etc.)

What Does Metabolism Have to Do with It All?

Well, I don't need to tell you that the sum of all chemical reactions within a living organism is what we refer to when we talk about metabolism in the physical scenario. It is indeed an imperative process for all forms of life – not just humans, existing from "womb to tomb." If metabolism stops, we *literally* die. We convert food into life energy when we consume it, and so, we convert life into meaning in a metaphorical sense. The life energy of the mind is 'meaning.' We are beings that create meaning. The metabolism of life into meaning also continues as we go about living our lives, just as physical metabolism does so without our knowledge.

Like in the body, there are many known and unknown factors that affect psychological metabolism, most of which are beyond our control. Meaning emerges into our awareness as we view and experience life. Human volition, as well as thought and emotion, are actually what's important. In the body, we experience symptoms that alert us to the fact that food is not being fully digested, allowing us to take enzymes, change our diet, or perform a series of tests to learn more. Similarly, we do not properly metabolize an event when we have symptoms in the psyche like worry, wrath, envy, or any other 'bad emotion' or undesirable behavior. Experience enhances our sense of completeness and our innate flow when it has been properly absorbed.

A healthy psychological metabolism will let you effectively process and cope with both positive and negative experiences and adapt to changing circumstances. It will allow you to maintain a balance of emotions and thoughts and to be resilient in the face of stress. For instance, you might have gone through a traumatic event in your life, such as a terrible car accident. After the event, you may experience a range of emotions, such as fear, anxiety, and sadness. Your psychological metabolism involves the way you process and copes with these emotions. If you would have a healthy psychological metabolism, you may engage in coping mechanisms such as talking to a therapist, adopting a different perspective toward life, and reaching out to friends and family for support. You may also be able to process the traumatic event and move forward in your life.

If, on the other hand, you have a poor psychological metabolism, you may struggle to cope with the emotions associated with the traumatic event. You may avoid dealing with the event and instead use maladaptive coping mechanisms such as substance abuse or withdrawing from social interactions, along with developing long-term mental health concerns. Remember that psychological metabolism is a complex process and can be influenced by various factors such as genetics, environment, and individual life experiences, and just like we all have different physical metabolisms, so do our minds!

Metabolize Your Strengths, Assets, And Abilities!

If you are wondering what I mean by metabolizing our strengths, I am referring to the process of taking our inherent strengths, assets, and abilities and using them to our advantage in order to achieve our goals and improve our overall happiness. We can do this by identifying our unique strengths and abilities and then using them in a purposeful and intentional way.

One way to metabolize our strengths is to think about the things that we enjoy doing and that come naturally to us. For instance, you can consider the things that you are good at and that others have complimented you on. Once you have identified these strengths, you can then use them to achieve your goals, whether that's in your personal or professional lives. For example, if one of your strengths is that you're good at organization, you can use that strength to plan and execute projects at work or manage an outing with your peers effectively.

It is also important to recognize that even though we have strengths and abilities, it's not always easy to use them. You may face challenges or obstacles that may prevent you from utilizing them fully…just like a puzzle. Each piece represents a unique strength, asset, or ability that you possess. Sometimes, it's easy to see how the pieces fit together, but other times, it may take a little more exploration and experimentation to find their place. Life can be challenging, like a tough puzzle too, and you may encounter obstacles that make it difficult to see how your strengths, assets, and abilities fit together. But with persistence and patience, you can find the right pieces and put them in their place to complete the puzzle.

Once that puzzle is complete, you'll be able to see the bigger picture and understand how all of your strengths, assets, and abilities work together to create a fulfilling and satisfying life. And just like a puzzle, you can always add more pieces and continue to build on what you have created. So, take the time to explore your strengths, assets, and abilities, and play around with how they fit together. It may take some effort and experimentation, but once you find the right pieces, you'll have a clear understanding of how they all work together to create the life you want.

Remember we talked about giving leverage to a young chef in his journey of mastering the skills? Well, let's bring that cooking skill back and think about metabolizing our skills, abilities, and strengths through that example again. And why not? We're talking about 'metabolism' after all.

Think of metabolizing your skills like cooking a delicious meal. Imagine you have all these amazing ingredients - your strong points, resources, skills, assets, and abilities - sitting in your pantry. But if you don't take them out, use them, and combine them in the right way, they're not going to do you much good, right?

Now just like a chef, you have to take those ingredients, understand their unique properties and how they work together, and then use them in a purposeful and intentional way to create a delicious meal. But unlike cooking, instead of a delicious meal, you'll be creating a delicious life!

Your strengths are like spices; they give the dish its unique flavor and make it stand out. Your assets are like the ingredients; they provide the foundation for the dish and give it structure. And your abilities are like the tools and techniques the chef uses to bring it all together. Just like how that young chef learned to experiment with different ingredients and techniques to create new and exciting dishes, you too can experiment with different ways to use your strengths, assets, and abilities to create a fulfilling and satisfying life.

So, it's time you don't let your strengths, assets, and abilities sit idly in the pantry; take them out, understand them, and use them to create the life you want. You'll be surprised at how delicious it will turn out to be!

Are You Ready to Embrace Yourself?

Do you realize how often we're always so hard on ourselves? We look in the mirror and pick out all our flaws or beat ourselves up over things we said or did that we regret. But here's the thing, we all have flaws; it's just a part of being human. And honestly, it's those imperfections that make us unique and special. So, why don't we try to accept ourselves just the way we are, with all our imperfections and flaws? Self-acceptance is all about being kind and understanding towards yourself instead of being harsh and judgmental.

It is the process of recognizing and acknowledging your own thoughts, feelings, and actions without judgment.

It's about recognizing that it's totally normal to make mistakes and that we're all just doing the best we can. When we practice self-acceptance, it can lead to improved mental health and well-being.

Moreover, it's important that we truthfully listen, respect, and have empathy for ourselves. It often happens that we put so much pressure and expectations on ourselves that we don't achieve the ultimate goal in our mind at the time we wanted, it starts to take a toll on us, and we begin to criticize ourselves. For instance, imagine that you are feeling overwhelmed with stress and anxiety about an upcoming work deadline. Instead of berating yourself for feeling this way or telling yourself to "Just pull yourself together!" you can take a moment to truly listen to your emotions and understand where they are coming from. You can then respect yourself by conceding that this is a difficult experience, task, or simply a tough schedule to manage, and have empathy for yourself by offering yourself kind and supportive words of encouragement. This can help to reduce feelings of stress and anxiety within yourself and will lead to a more positive and self-compassionate response.

Also, in difficult times like these, always recall your past successes and how you managed everything. In doing so, try to keep in mind the difference in circumstances and how you can tweak your style, being kind to yourself all along. Remember that identifying and drawing upon past successes and communicating confidence in the same are closely related. You can reflect on your accomplishments and identify patterns of what you've done well in the past. This process will help you to understand your fortes, skills, and capabilities and give you a sense of what you're capable of achieving. Ultimately, it will serve as a source of inspiration and motivation to help you tackle new challenges and achieve new goals.

Communicating confidence by expressing belief in yourself and your abilities helps in building confidence in yourself and communicating that confidence to others as well. Doing so gives others a sense of your capabilities as well as the potential for your future success. Let me explain it to you this way.

Imagine you're going on a treasure hunt. You've got a map in your hand, and you're on the lookout for clues that will lead you to the treasure. The treasure in this scenario represents your past successes, and the clues represent the things you've done well in the past.

As you embark on your treasure hunt, you'll come across various obstacles and challenges, but you'll also find clues that will guide you toward the treasure. These clues may come in the form of the lessons learned, the small victories achieved in the past, positive feedback, or even small wins. As you collect more and more clues, you'll start to see a clearer picture of where the treasure is hidden.

Once you've gathered enough clues, you'll be able to identify your former achievements (the treasure in this case) and draw upon them to help guide you toward your goals. And just like how a treasure hunter communicates confidence in their abilities and the direction they're heading, you too can communicate confidence in yourself and your abilities by highlighting your earlier feats.

Focus on your efforts, progress forward, and don't let any bad thoughts ruin the treasure path you created with zeal and zest. Concentrating and realizing your efforts will help you in generating alternatives for disheartening unreal beliefs and oppressive narratives. When we focus on our efforts, we are able to see the progress we have made and the progress we can make in the future. This shift in perspective can help us to see things in a more positive light and can help to counter disheartening and oppressive thoughts and beliefs. For example, if you have a belief that you're not good enough, focusing on your efforts can help you see that you have been working hard and making progress rather than focusing on the end result or outcome. This shift in focus can help you to recognize that you are capable of achieving your goals and can help to counteract the belief that you're not good enough.

Similarly, oppressive narratives can create feelings of helplessness and hopelessness, but by focusing on our hard work, we can see that we have agency and that we can take action to change our circumstances. It allows us to emphasize what is in control rather than getting stuck in feelings of helplessness and hopelessness.

The journey to embracing yourself, savoring the moments, realizing your strengths, and focusing on your hard work can be tough as it requires facing personal challenges and overcoming internal obstacles, but with patience, understanding, and consistent effort, it can turn out to be a rewarding and empowering process.

Chapter 8: Your 'Why' & 'Oath' in Life

"When life's purpose is clear, even the toughest obstacles become bearable, for a strong 'why' fuels the strength to overcome any 'how'."

Have you ever found yourself going through the motions of life without really understanding the purpose behind your actions? It's a common feeling, but one that can leave us feeling unfulfilled and lacking direction. That's where the power of 'why' comes in. Understanding the reason behind what we do can bring a new level of meaning and motivation to our lives. As we navigate through life, it's easy to get caught up in the day-to-day tasks and responsibilities that fill our days. But if we stop and ask ourselves the fundamental questions of why we are doing what we do and what our ultimate purpose is, we can tap into a deeper meaning and fulfillment.

Have you ever used a compass with a needle pointing in the right direction when you're lost? If yes, you must know very well how it feels to be lost and then hold onto that beacon of hope that you might just end up where you want to be by following that path that the compass is pointing in.

Just like that, having a purpose in your life can be compared to having a compass in a vast sea of possibilities. Just like a compass point you in the right direction and helps you navigate your journey, a sense of purpose can give you direction, meaning, and motivation in life. It's like having a map that guides you toward your unique destination, where you can fully realize your potential and live a life filled with passion and fulfillment. A study found that having a sense of purpose in life can help individuals cope with daily stressors. The study followed nearly 2,000 middle-aged adults for eight days and found a positive correlation between having a sense of purpose and better stress management. The findings suggest that having a clear purpose in life can serve as a protective factor against the negative effects of stress.[25]

Another study by the same researchers in a different journal investigated the relationship between having a sense of purpose and earning money. The results of the study suggested that individuals with a strong sense of purpose tend to have better work performance and higher income levels compared to those without a strong sense of purpose. The study supported the idea that having a clear purpose in life can influence an individual's motivation and drive in various aspects of their life, including their career and financial success.[26]

Furthermore, another study explored the relationship between social media feedback (in this case, 'likes' on Facebook) and self-esteem. The study found that having a sense of purpose can diminish the effect of social media feedback on an individual's self-worth.[27] Particularly, people with a strong feeling of purpose were less susceptible to the number of Facebook likes they received than those without a sense of purpose. This suggests that having a clear sense of purpose can provide a source of stability and resilience, helping us to maintain a more stable sense of self-worth and to be less influenced by external validation.

Picture yourself as a painter, with your purpose as the masterpiece you're trying to create. Every decision you make, and every action you take, is like a stroke of the brush, adding to the beauty and richness of the painting. As you bring your purpose to life, you'll find that you are living in flow, with a sense of joy and direction. And in the end, you'll be proud to have created a life that truly reflects who you are and what you stand for.

The 'why,' which is our purpose in life, provides us with a reason to exist and drives our actions. The purpose is often rooted in our values and beliefs, which serve as the guiding principles for making decisions and shaping behavior. However, sometimes our beliefs can become so deeply ingrained that we don't stop to question whether they are even true or not. This is where the process of evaluation comes in. To evaluate our beliefs, we must be willing to step back and take a critical look at them. We should ask ourselves if what we believe is based on facts and evidence or simply our own biases and preconceived notions. This can be a difficult process, as it requires us to be open-minded and willing to accept the possibility that we may be wrong.

Another important question to ask ourselves is what we are living for or what we are running after. Are we putting our time, energy, and effort into things that truly matter? Or are we simply going through the motions, following a path that we think we're supposed to be on, but it's actually not even the true path? If we're not sure what the right path is, it's okay to seek out guidance and learn new things.

When faced with challenges and difficulties, having a strong sense of purpose and an unwavering commitment to the right values can provide a source of motivation and resilience, helping us to persevere and continue to live a better life. For example, while playing a sport, you may be motivated by values such as competition, friendship, connectedness, winning, and challenge.

However, participating in sports often involves being exposed to and experiencing setbacks and losses. In these situations, having a clear sense of why you are playing the sport and connecting with your values can provide a source of resilience and motivation to continue, even in the face of adversity. This highlights the importance of understanding and connecting with your values and purpose in life.

For instance, if you ask yourself, *why do I play baseball?* You can come to realize you do it for a lot of things that you didn't realize at one point because you never paid attention to your 'why.' You may play baseball for the love of competition, to build and maintain friendships, to feel connected to a community, to experience the thrill of winning, or to push yourself to overcome challenges. Once you understand the values and beliefs that underlie your love for baseball, you can use them to stay motivated and focused, even in the face of adversity or setbacks.

Or, you can ask yourself, *why do I go to college?* Realizing your purpose for going to college can involve understanding the values and goals that drive your decision to pursue higher education. Your underlying values for going to college can involve getting an education, learning new things, attaining novel feats, making relationships, acquiring knowledge, developing new skills, increasing your career opportunities, achieving financial stability, fulfilling your personal passion, or contributing to society in meaningful ways. Your values can go in way more diverse directions depending upon your perspective because, at the end of the day, college is truly a learning experience not only academically but personally as well. We are tried and tested, and more often than not, we come up short. Falling back on our values and why we are at college motivates us to dig deep through inevitable challenges.

Or, you can even ask yourself, *why do I go to therapy?* You can realize you go for psychological help to address mental health concerns, to cope with difficult life events, to improve relationships, to gain self-awareness and personal growth, or to achieve a sense of well-being. By connecting with your purpose, you can stay motivated and focused on your goals for therapy and work more effectively with your therapist to achieve the outcomes you desire.

Our values and purpose not only help in our academic, professional, or sports life but also in our personal lives, such as connecting with our family. If you are a parent, you can understand that being a parent is a rewarding experience, but at the same time, it is challenging too. Falling back on our 'why' and values can re-energize us and prevent us from quitting. When faced with obstacles, it can be helpful to remember why you started and what is important to you, which can help you stay absorbed and committed to your goals.

It's not easy to compete for ourselves or others, whether it's school, work, sports, relationships, or parenthood…we expose ourselves to all. It is challenging and puts a lot of pressure on us. Having a clear understanding of our values and purpose can serve as a source of strength and inspiration, and that is why our WHY is so important.

When we participate in activities that are not mandatory, such as sports or hobbies, we often have a greater emotional investment in them compared to activities that are mandatory, such as work or school. These non-mandatory activities can make us feel more vulnerable and exposed to disappointment or failure. Having a clear understanding of our values and purpose, our 'why' can provide a sense of resilience and help us to better handle challenges and setbacks, as it can serve as a reminder of our priorities and what is truly important to us. Similarly, marriage and being a parent are choices that we often make ourselves. Again, people do so, and in these aspects, we are often very vulnerable.

What's your Why?

Why are you a parent?

Why do you play baseball?

Why do you go to college?

Why do you go to therapy?

Why do you choose to eat healthy food?

Why do you go for a walk every day?

Understanding your values, purpose, and motivations, or 'why,' is an important aspect of overall well-being. Here are some steps that can help you uncover your 'why' and make your life better:

- ***Reflect on your values:*** Think about what is truly important to you, what you stand for, and what you believe in. If not sure, search for the truth and gauge those values and beliefs to find out if they are even right for yourself or not.

- ***Identify your passions:*** What do you love to do? What activities bring you joy and energy?

- ***Consider your unique strengths and skills:*** What are you naturally good at? What comes easily to you?

- ***Think about what you want to contribute to the world:*** What positive impact do you want to make? What kind of legacy do you want to leave?

- ***Visualize your ideal life:*** Imagine what your life would look like if you were living your 'why.' How would you feel? What would you be doing?

Once you have a clearer understanding of your 'why,' you can start making changes to align your life with your purpose.

Oath to Self – A Game Changer!

An oath or a promise made to oneself is often a declaration of their intentions, values, or principles. Oaths made to ourselves can be important because they serve as a means of self-commitment and accountability. By making an oath, you affirm your beliefs and values and declare your intent to act in accordance with them. This can help to build character, encourage personal growth, and create a sense of responsibility to yourself and others. Personal oaths can also provide a sense of purpose and direction, helping you to stay focused on your goals and aspirations. In my opinion, oaths are very intricate commitments and should be valiantly pursued.

Moreover, making a promise to yourself at its core, serves as an ultimate coping mechanism to combat automatic thoughts that we discussed in previous chapters. Personal oaths can help in combating automatic thoughts by providing a clear and intentional declaration of values, beliefs, and aspirations. When you make a personal oath, you establish a conscious commitment to live in a specific way, and this can serve as a reminder to counteract negative automatic thoughts that may arise. You can use it as a reference point when you experience negative or self-doubt thoughts. The oath serves as a reminder of your values and intentions and will help to reframe automatic thoughts in a more positive and productive way.

If we talk about coping thoughts, they are mental strategies that we can use to manage negative thoughts and emotions that arise in response to a triggering situation. By thinking differently about a situation, we can change our emotional response to it. In this regard, personal oaths can serve as a framework for developing coping thoughts that are aligned with our values and beliefs. For example, if you have made an oath to yourself to always see the best in others, you can use this as a coping thought when faced with a situation that challenges this belief. By reframing your thoughts to align with your oath, you can change your emotional response to the situation and feel differently about it.

Personal oaths are like a secret weapon for supercharging your life! They're like the ultimate "cheat code" for becoming the best version of yourself. By taking an oath, you're basically making a promise to yourself to do something you feel is right or become a better version of yourself, even when nobody's watching. And, let's be real, that's pretty cool. Plus, it's a super easy way to step up your game and show the world what you're made of, and that's the reason I call it a game-changer!

What's The Relation between My 'Why' and My 'Oath'?

Personal oaths and 'why' in life are closely related because they both serve as a guiding force for an individual's actions and decisions. The 'why' in life refers to an individual's purpose, values, and beliefs that drive their behavior and shape their goals. An oath made to oneself can serve as a tangible expression of these values and beliefs and provide a way to hold oneself accountable to them. When you take an oath, you are making a deliberate commitment to align your actions with your 'why' and to strive toward your life's purpose.

Having a strong 'Why' and 'Oath' can optimize our performance because we can surely find strength in discomfort. Think of it like this. Imagine you're a long-distance runner in a race. The going gets tough, and you're starting to feel fatigued, but you're reminded of your 'why' - maybe it's to inspire others or raise money for a cause you're passionate about. That 'why,' that purpose, is what drives you forward, giving you the strength to push through the discomfort and continue running. And that oath you made to yourself, to give your best and never give up, is like a sturdy pair of running shoes, providing stability and support to help you maintain your pace. With your why and oath guiding you, you are able to optimize your performance and cross the finish line with pride and accomplishment.

Just like this in life, having a strong why and oath can provide the motivation and resolve to overcome challenges and reach your goals. By having a firm belief in your 'why,' and by being committed to it, we are able to make adjustments and swivel as a result of our mistakes or errors. We don't let mistakes own us!

I would like you to understand this by thinking about a lighthouse in a stormy sea. It provides a constant source of guidance and direction, even when the winds of change are blowing, and the waves of challenges are crashing. When you have a firm belief in your 'why,' it gives you the resilience and determination to keep moving forward, even when things don't go as planned.

For instance, if you're on a mission to climb a mountain and you encounter obstacles along the way, you might need to adjust your route, find new tools, or seek help from others. As long as your 'why' is strong enough, you won't give up on your goal. Instead, you'll find creative ways to overcome the obstacles and keep moving toward the summit. Similarly, in life and business, we all make mistakes and encounter obstacles. But if we have a strong sense of our 'why' and remain committed to it, we can use those setbacks as opportunities to pivot and find new and better ways to achieve our goals.

If you're looking for a spark to ignite your purpose and drive, look no further than the relationship between personal oaths and the 'why' in your life! This dynamic duo is like gasoline and fire, just waiting to fuel your journey to greatness. The 'why' in life is your ultimate motivation, the reason you get up in the morning, the fire in your belly that pushes you forward. An oath made to oneself is like the rocket fuel that propels you towards that 'why' with unyielding force. It's your commitment to stay true to your values and beliefs, no matter what life throws your way. When you bring these two together, you've got a recipe for a life that's truly extraordinary!

Chapter 9: The Other Side

Her heart was shattered; a million pieces spread
The love she gave, now nothing but dead
But still, she stood, a smile on her face
Hiding the tears, and the lonely embrace

She walked the streets with a head held high
Pretending that everything was just fine
But inside, she was broken, her soul in a daze
As she faced a world filled with heartache and blaze

Yet she was strong; she wouldn't give in
She'd face this heartbreak with a smile and a grin
For she knew that with time, she'd heal and grow
And the love that once shattered would someday glow.

Pause for a moment and let the above words sink in. If you have undergone similar circumstances in your life, I don't need to explain the vivid picture painted in the above poetry of a person who has experienced heartbreak but is determined to keep moving forward with a brave face. It captures the raw emotions of a person who has suffered a loss but is determined not to let it define their story.

The clear picture of the pain and struggle that the person is going through is evident, yet, despite this, she is able to hold her head high. Do you realize how even in the darkest moments, we have the power to rise above the pain and keep moving forward? This is what I call the 'other side.' The other side embodies optimism over pessimism. As we navigate through life's ups and downs, would we want to be remembered as the protagonist or the antagonist?

Optimists are more prospective to see opportunities for growth and find meaning in stressful experiences compared to pessimists.[28] As per research, the differences between optimists and pessimists may be influenced by the way they focus their attention. Studies have shown that when presented with both positive and negative stimuli, optimists tend to pay more attention to the positive, while pessimists tend to pay more attention to the negative. This difference in attentional processes may contribute to the observed differences in outlook between these two groups.[29] This indicates that a negative individual may concentrate more on the bad or dangerous parts of certain circumstances while neglecting the good or motivating aspects.

Being optimistic has its perks, especially when it comes to handling life's challenges. An optimistic individual has the ability to see both the bright and the dark side of a situation. They don't just focus on the negatives; they take in all the information, the good and the bad, and use it to create a comprehensive understanding of the situation to form their other side. This type of outlook is like having a 360-degree view of life. When you have another side perspective, you're more likely to find meaning and growth in stressful experiences. After all, how can you grow from a situation if you only see half of it?

Think of the other side like assembling a puzzle. An optimist has all the pieces, both the positive and negative, and uses them to build a complete picture. The more pieces you have, the more accurate and valuable the picture becomes. The same goes for life.

By seeing all the pieces, the optimist is more likely to turn a negative experience into a positive one and find growth and meaning in it. Furthermore, an optimist is more likely to approach the future with hope and excitement, even in the face of challenges and setbacks.

Please note that being optimistic does not mean constantly being overly positive or denying negative emotions. Rather, it is about the way we attribute the events and experiences in our lives. An optimistic thinking style involves seeing the causes of our experiences in a more favorable light, focusing on the positive aspects and potential opportunities rather than dwelling solely on the negatives.[30] This type of outlook helps to maintain a more balanced and hopeful view of life, even in the face of challenges and setbacks.

People with an optimistic thinking style possess a unique perspective that enables them to embrace the negatives as stepping stones toward growth. Rather than being discouraged by setbacks, they view them as invaluable opportunities for self-reflection and learning. By carefully examining what went wrong, optimists gain profound insights that propel them forward on their journey. They understand that the path to success is often paved with lessons learned from failures. Thus, optimists choose to extract wisdom from the negatives, harnessing their transformative power to fuel their continued optimism and resilience.

The way individuals interpret positive and negative events is influenced by three factors: Personalization, Permanence, and Pervasiveness.[31] Personalization refers to whether an individual views the cause of an event as being within their control or beyond their control. Permanence refers to whether they see the outcome as being permanent or temporary. Pervasiveness refers to the extent to which an individual sees the event as having a broad impact on their life, regardless of context or, if it is specific to a particular situation.

By considering these factors, individuals can gain a better understanding of their reactions to events and develop a more positive outlook. For example, if an individual perceives the cause of a negative event as being temporary and specific to a particular situation rather than a permanent and pervasive part of their life, they are more likely to see the event in a positive light and find opportunities for growth and development. On the other hand, if they view the event as being permanent and beyond their control, they may be more likely to become stuck in a negative mindset and struggle to find a positive outcome. We can look at an interesting example of personalization, permanence, and pervasiveness by looking at how people react to rejection in romantic relationships.

First, let's consider personalization. When someone is rejected by a romantic partner, they may interpret the situation as being within their control or beyond their control. For example, if they blame themselves for the rejection, they may see it as a personal failure and feel like they are not good enough. On the other side, if they believe that external factors played a role in the rejection (such as the other person's preferences or circumstances), they may not take it as personally and may be more likely to move on.

Next, let's look at permanence. Rejection can feel particularly painful because it can be perceived as a permanent outcome. People may feel like they will never find love again or that they will always be alone. This feeling of permanence can make the rejection feel even more devastating and difficult to cope with. However, while rejection may feel permanent, intensifying the pain, it's important to view that permanence brings stability and consistency, allowing us to focus on self-love and personal growth. It redirects us towards better paths and opens doors to new possibilities.

Finally, let's examine pervasiveness. Rejection can be a pervasive experience, affecting how people view themselves and their ability to form and maintain relationships. A person who has been rejected may begin to question their worth, their attractiveness, or their ability to connect with others. This can lead to a negative spiral where they may feel more hesitant to pursue romantic relationships in the future, leading to further rejection and reinforcing their negative beliefs about themselves.

However, it's important to note that pervasiveness can also have a positive aspect. By acknowledging and addressing the negative beliefs, individuals can embark on a journey of self-discovery and personal growth. Through self-reflection and resilience, they can develop a stronger sense of self, cultivate healthier relationships, and foster a positive outlook on themselves and their ability to connect with others.

To tie all of this together, if someone blames themselves for the rejection of a romantic partner (personalization), they may feel like they will never find love again (permanence) and begin to question their worth as a partner (pervasiveness). On the other side, if they see the rejection as being due to external factors (personalization), they may be able to move on more easily and see the situation as temporary (permanence) without it having a pervasive impact on their sense of self (pervasiveness).

As you can see in the explanation of the concept above that, change of perspective played a great role here, i.e., change of view from pessimism to optimism. However, among the tons of benefits of optimistic thinking, it is important to be attentive, practical, and aware; else, optimism can also be problematic when taken to an extreme. When people become too optimistic, it can lead to a form of reality avoidance where they become attached to unrealistic self-delusions and idealistic views. This can result in ignoring warning signs or potential problems and a tendency to be overly optimistic about future outcomes. Optimism can be like a double-edged sword. On the one hand, it can help us stay motivated and see the best in a situation, but on the other side, if not utilized practically, it can blind us to reality and prevent us from taking necessary precautions or making realistic preparations. So, it's important to strike a balance between being optimistic and realistic to ensure that our outlook on life remains grounded and well-informed.

The Link Between Optimism, Mental & Physical Health, and Longevity

Let me get straight to the point: various studies that have examined the relationship between optimism and mental health outcomes, such as depression, anxiety, and stress, reveal that optimism is associated with lower levels of psychological distress and better coping skills.[32] Additionally, optimism can be a protective factor against the negative impact of stress on physical health.

As a matter of fact, when we experience stress, our bodies release stress hormones, such as cortisol and adrenaline, as part of the body's fight-or-flight response. This response prepares the body to respond to perceived threats or danger, but if it is activated too frequently or for too long, it can lead to negative health consequences such as high blood pressure, weakened immune system, and even chronic diseases. Optimism can act as a protective factor against the negative impact of stress on physical health in several ways. Firstly, optimists are more likely to perceive stressful situations as challenges rather than threats. They tend to have a positive outlook on the future and believe that they can overcome challenges. This optimistic mindset can help reduce the physiological response to stress and prevent the release of excessive stress hormones that can harm the body.

Secondly, optimists are more likely to engage in proactive coping strategies to manage stress. They may seek social support, engage in physical exercise, or practice relaxation techniques, which can help reduce the impact of stress on the body. This proactive approach can help break the cycle of stress and prevent negative health consequences.

The relationships underlying optimism and constructive behaviors have been examined in different studies. In view of the foregoing, the research found that optimism was associated with healthy lifestyles such as cessation of smoking, consuming alcohol in moderation, developing a routine of walking quickly, and regularly engaging in physical activity, irrespective of demographic factors, present developmental conditions, or mass index.[33]

Let's have a deeper look at mental health, physical health, and longevity from an optimistic perspective one by one.

- **Optimism's Impact on Mental Wellbeing**

Optimism and mental health are strongly intertwined, and cultivating a positive outlook can have a significant impact on your mental well-being. Let's dive in and explore this connection together!

Firstly, let's continue to define optimism. Optimism is a way of thinking that focuses on the positive aspects of life and expects positive outcomes. It's about viewing challenges as opportunities for growth and believing that things will work out in the end. Now, let's look at mental health. Mental health refers to our emotional, psychological, and social well-being. It affects how we think, feel, and act and influences our ability to cope with the ups and downs of life.

So, how are these two concepts related? Well, research has shown that people who are optimistic tend to have better mental health outcomes. They are more resilient in the face of adversity, cope better with stress, and have lower rates of depression and anxiety. Optimism can also help us to build stronger relationships, be more productive, and feel more motivated to pursue our goals.

On the other hand, pessimism, or a negative outlook on life, can have a detrimental effect on our mental health. It can lead to feelings of hopelessness, anxiety, and depression and make it harder to cope with the challenges that life throws our way. Pessimistic thinking can also cause us to give up on our goals and withdraw from social situations, leading to feelings of isolation and loneliness.

Even research has discovered an inverse relationship between optimism and suicidal tendencies, as well as depressive symptoms.[34] As a result, optimism appears to play a significant mitigating effect in the relationship underlying suicide notions and feelings of hopelessness.[35]

It is important to focus on the positive, challenge negative thoughts, surround ourselves with positivity, and take care of ourselves. Remember, a little optimism can go a long way!

- ## Impact of Optimism on Physical Wellbeing

Optimism and physical health are closely related, and having a positive outlook on life can have a significant impact on your physical well-being. We already discussed what optimism is, so now, let's look at physical health. Physical health refers to the state of our body and its ability to function properly. It affects our energy levels, immunity, and overall quality of life.

Now let's explore the connection between the two. Research has shown that compared to pessimism, optimism is associated with greater physical health. Additionally, pessimism is linked to an excess of somatic complaints, in stark comparison to positivity.[36]

People who are optimistic tend to have better physical health outcomes. Optimism can boost our immune system, lower our risk of chronic diseases such as heart disease and diabetes, and even help us to live longer. Moreover, optimistic people are also more likely to engage in healthy behaviors such as exercise, healthy eating, and getting enough sleep, which can have a positive impact on physical health.

On the other hand, pessimism, or a negative outlook on life, can have a detrimental effect on our physical health. Pessimistic thinking can lead to chronic stress, which is associated with a range of health problems, including high blood pressure, heart disease, and depression.

One of the most impressive impacts of optimism on physical health is its ability to boost our immune system. Studies have shown that optimistic individuals have stronger immune responses to infections and are less likely to get sick. One notable study was conducted by researchers at the

University of Kentucky,[37] where the researchers recruited 124 law students who were scheduled to take their final exams. The students were given a questionnaire to assess their level of optimism and then provided saliva samples to measure levels of immunoglobulin A (IgA), an antibody that helps to protect against upper respiratory infections. The results showed that students who were more optimistic had higher levels of IgA in their saliva, indicating a stronger immune response. In addition, the more optimistic students reported fewer symptoms of illness during the exam period, and their symptoms were less severe than those of their less optimistic peers.

Additionally, having a positive outlook can increase the activity of natural killer cells, which are part of the immune system that fights off viruses and cancer. It can also enhance the production of antibodies, which help to protect us from infectious diseases. Moreover, people with a positive outlook on life have been shown to have lower rates of heart disease and other cardiovascular problems. A study published in the journal Psychosomatic Medicine found that women who scored higher on optimism measures had lower levels of inflammation, a key contributor to heart disease.[38] Optimism has a truly remarkable impact on our physical well-being. From boosting our immune system to improving our heart health, the benefits of maintaining an optimistic outlook are truly impressive.

- **Impact of Optimism on Longevity**

Have you ever heard the phrase 'looking on the bright side of life'? It turns out that this outlook on life might be more than just a positive attitude; it could actually help you live longer. Researchers have been studying the link between optimism and longevity for decades, and the evidence is clear: people who have a more optimistic outlook on life tend to live longer than those who are more pessimistic.

So, how exactly are longevity and optimism related? One theory is the same as we discussed earlier - better-coping skills with stress and adversity. Another theory is that optimistic people are more likely to take care of themselves.[39] People who believe that good things will happen to them in the future are more likely to engage in healthy behaviors, such as eating a balanced diet, getting regular exercise, and avoiding risky behaviors like smoking and excessive drinking. In fact, studies have shown that optimistic people are more likely to follow through with healthy habits than those who are more pessimistic. For example, a study published in the Journal of Personality and

Social Psychology found that people who scored higher on measures of optimism were more likely to quit smoking than those who scored lower.[40]

Of course, it's important to remember that optimism alone is not a magic bullet for living longer. It's just one of many factors that contribute to overall health and well-being. However, cultivating an optimistic outlook on life can be a powerful tool for improving your overall quality of life and increasing your chances of a long and healthy life.

From Dream to Reality - How Optimism Helps Turn Ambition into Achievement?

Let me share with you something truly remarkable about the power of expectations. What we expect to happen in our lives can determine the course of our actions, our level of effort, and, ultimately, the outcome we achieve.

Have you ever stopped to think about how much our expectations shape our lives? From the big decisions we make about our careers and relationships to the everyday choices we make about what to eat or wear, our expectations are the foundation of everything we do. When we have high expectations, we set our sights on achieving great things. We challenge ourselves to reach for the stars, to be the best we can be, and to leave our mark on the world. We believe that we can do anything we set our minds to and that conviction fuels our passion and our drive. But when our expectations are low, we limit ourselves. We settle for less than we deserve, and we hold ourselves back from reaching our full potential. We convince ourselves that we can't achieve our goals, and we give up before we even try.

When you're optimistic about the future, you tend to set ambitious goals and work tirelessly to achieve them. Your positive expectations give you the motivation and drive to take risks, overcome obstacles, and persevere through difficult times. You believe in yourself, your abilities, and your potential, and that belief fuels your success. On the flip side, when you hold negative expectations about your future, it's easy to become discouraged and disheartened. You might choose not to pursue challenging goals because you don't believe you can achieve them. You might put in minimal effort because you don't think it will make a difference. And when things don't go as planned, you might be quick to give up and abandon your dreams.

It's important to understand that our expectations are not set in stone. We have the power to shape them, and in turn, they shape us. By choosing to adopt a more positive outlook on life, we can unlock a world of possibilities and achieve more than we ever thought possible. Even research endorses it, claiming that organizing the main objective well before an event, increases the possibility that a favorable outcome will be obtained, which is the first appealed advantage of optimistic expectations.[41]

For example, imagine you are preparing for a job interview. If you hold optimistic expectations about the interview, you are more likely to prepare thoroughly and put in the effort needed to present yourself in the best possible light. This increased effort and preparation can lead to better performance in the interview and ultimately increase the likelihood of receiving a job offer. On the other hand, if you have pessimistic expectations about the interview, you may not prepare as thoroughly or put in as much effort, which could negatively impact your performance and decrease the likelihood of a job offer.

When thinking positively in situations like these, increased effort and persistence can lead to greater success and achievement. When you pursue your goals with optimism and determination, you may be more likely to overcome obstacles and persevere in the face of setbacks. You may also be more willing to take risks and try new approaches, which can lead to innovation and creativity.

However, as it is said, "Too much of a good thing is a bad thing," implying that even things that are generally positive or beneficial can become harmful or negative when taken to excess. For example, while exercise is generally good for health, too much exercise can lead to injuries and burnout. Similarly, while certain foods may be enjoyable, too much indulgence can lead to weight gain and health problems. The same is the case here with optimism. One study suggests that while optimistic expectations can lead to greater effort and positive emotions, they can also be associated with a decreased ability to adjust to negative outcomes.[42] The study conducted a series of experiments to examine the relationship between optimistic expectations and effort, emotion, and outcome adjustment and found that individuals with optimistic expectations tended to put in more effort and experience more positive emotions when pursuing a goal.

However, the study also found that when faced with negative outcomes, individuals with optimistic expectations were less likely to adjust their expectations and were more likely to experience negative emotions. Overall, the study suggested that while optimistic expectations can have benefits for effort and emotion, individuals should also be prepared to adjust their expectations in response to negative outcomes.

And let's be real for a moment. Life is full of twists and turns, and things don't always go according to plan. Despite this, if we continue to believe in our overly optimistic expectations even when reality tells us otherwise, it can lead to disappointment, frustration, and a sense of failure when those expectations aren't met.

So why do we fall into this trap of optimism bias? It's because optimism feels good. It makes us feel empowered and gives us a sense of control over our lives. And while some degree of optimism can be helpful, too much can be detrimental. You can think of it like a parachute. Just as a parachute helps you safely land after a jump, having realistic expectations helps you navigate life's challenges with a sense of balance and stability. If your expectations are too high, it's like jumping out of a plane with a faulty parachute - you may be in for a rough landing. But if your expectations are realistic and grounded in reality, it's like having a reliable parachute to carry you through life's ups and downs.

All-in-all, holding optimistic expectations about the future can serve as a powerful catalyst for goal pursuit and achievement. Like in a race, you have a finish line that you want to reach, and you need to exert effort and overcome obstacles to get there. Optimistic expectations help you set the pace, stay motivated, and push through the difficulties of the race. It's like having an internal cheering crowd, giving you the encouragement and support you need to cross the finish line!

Optimism at Work

Imagine walking into a workplace where employees are highly motivated, collaborative, and consistently exceed expectations. As an employer, this is the dream scenario.

But how do you create an environment that fosters such a positive and productive workforce? While there are many factors that can impact employee performance, one of the most important is optimism. The way employees think and feel about their work, and the organization they work for can have a profound effect on their motivation, creativity, and overall performance.

Did you know that optimistic employees are more likely to outperform their pessimistic counterparts?

A study conducted by the University of Pennsylvania found that optimistic salespeople sold 37% more than their pessimistic peers.[43] Additionally, optimistic employees are more resilient to stress, less likely to experience burnout, and have better mental health overall.

These impressive findings demonstrate just how much of an impact optimism can have on employee performance.

Different factors influence employee performance at work, one of which is the work culture. Think of work culture as a sailboat and employees as crew members. The optimistic work culture is like favorable winds and calm seas that allow the sailboat to move quickly and efficiently toward its destination. In contrast, negative work culture is like strong headwinds and turbulent waves that make it difficult for the sailboat to make progress and may even cause it to capsize. In an optimistic work culture, employees feel empowered and motivated to perform at their best. They are given the tools and resources they need to succeed, and their achievements are recognized and celebrated. This creates a positive feedback loop where employees feel valued and appreciated, leading to increased motivation, higher productivity, and better outcomes. However, negative work culture can create a toxic environment that undermines employee confidence and creates unnecessary obstacles. In such a culture, employees may feel unsupported, overworked, and unappreciated, leading to decreased motivation, lower productivity, and poor performance. Just like a sailboat needs a supportive crew to navigate the seas successfully, employees need a positive work culture to achieve their full potential.

A strong work culture that fosters optimism creates a sense of community and shared purpose, leading to better teamwork, collaboration, and communication. Optimism and a positive mindset are vital to overcoming the challenges and inevitable hurdles that life often presents to us. Our outlook on life, and the beliefs we hold about ourselves and our capabilities, can significantly impact our success and happiness. While it may not always be easy to maintain an optimistic outlook, especially when faced with adversity, we must remember that our mindset is within our control. With a little effort and determination, we can choose to cultivate a positive and optimistic mindset, which can help us navigate through even the toughest of times. And with that, we move onward, charged with the knowledge that our mindset is a powerful tool that can help us achieve our goals and live the life we deserve!

Chapter 10: Personal Courage

"Courage surpasses innate skills; it thrives in the audacity to venture into the unknown, embracing risks and defying uncertainties that life presents."

What if I mess this up? What if I'm not good enough to close the deal I have been working tirelessly to secure for months?

What if I'm not smart enough to pass this exam? What if I can't remember anything?

What if I can't keep up with my friends? I'm not strong enough. Why did I even think I could hike a mountain?

The thoughts…the judgments…the fear of being imperfect…the fear of being a failure…we all have it, don't we? It's that nagging feeling that we're not good enough, that we don't measure up to some impossible standard of perfection. But here's the thing: perfection is a myth. It's like a unicorn, a mythical creature that we all chase but can never catch. Sure, we all want to be successful, loved, and respected. And there's nothing wrong with that. But the truth is, no one is perfect. We all have flaws and imperfections.

The fear of imperfection can hold us back from experiencing the great adventures of life. This fear can be so paralyzing that it can prevent us from pursuing our passions, taking risks, and achieving our goals. But what if I told you that imperfection is not something to be feared but something to be embraced? That's right! We're not meant to be perfect, and that's what makes us unique and interesting.

Think about it - if we were all perfect, what would there be left to aspire to? What would be left to learn, to explore, and to discover? Imperfection is what makes life exciting and full of surprises. It's what allows us to grow and evolve as individuals, to push ourselves beyond our limits, and to achieve greatness. It's what gives us a chance to learn, adapt, and improve. But acknowledging our flaws and limitations takes a special kind of courage - a courage that many of us struggle to muster. Accepting our imperfections means facing our vulnerabilities head-on, being honest with ourselves about our strengths and weaknesses, and accommodating the fact that we're all a work in progress. And make no mistake - this kind of bravery is not for the faint of heart.

But the payoff is immeasurable. When we embrace our imperfections, we open ourselves up to a world of possibility. We can take risks, try new things, and push ourselves to new heights. Remember, true courage is not found in avoiding challenges or seeking an easy way out but rather in facing problems head-on and persevering through them. It is easy to be a critic and sit on the sidelines, but it takes courage to step into the arena of life and actively engage with the challenges that come our way.

Let's understand this concept through an example. Let's say you and your best friend have had a falling out over a misunderstanding. It's easy to avoid the issue and let the friendship fade away, but it takes real courage to confront the problem and work toward a resolution. So, you decide to take the first step by reaching out to your friend to schedule a time to talk. It's nerve-wracking, but you know it's the right thing to do.

When you finally sit down to talk, it's uncomfortable at first, but you both make an effort to listen to each other and share your feelings honestly. It's not an easy conversation, but as you talk, you start to see each other's perspectives and realize that the misunderstanding was just that - a miscommunication. You apologize for any hurt feelings you may have caused, and your friend apologizes as well. You both commit to working on the friendship and finding ways to strengthen it moving forward.

It takes true courage to face difficult conversations and work through problems in a friendship, but by doing so, you can ultimately become stronger and better equipped to navigate future challenges in your life. And this type of courage is what we refer to as 'personal courage.'

Personal Courage

Have you ever found yourself in a situation where you had to muster up the nerve to face a challenge? Initially, you might think about a person intervening in a situation where someone is being harassed or a man running into a burning building to help a person in need. These are examples of general courage, the kind that helps us navigate through the external dangers and challenges that we may face in our daily lives.

But what about personal courage? This is the kind of courage that is required to face the internal challenges and obstacles that we encounter on our journey of personal growth and development. It's the courage that allows us to confront our deepest fears, acknowledge our weaknesses, and work on improving ourselves. While society often associates courage with daring physical feats like climbing a mountain or battling a deadly animal, true courage stems from our inner strength to face and overcome obstacles, and that's what we are talking about here!

Courage is often perceived as an attribute of heroes or brave individuals who demonstrate fearlessness in the face of great danger. However, it is not just a quality that is reserved for the few but can be practiced and developed by anyone, anywhere, and at any time. It's something that allows a person to take a challenging exam or try something new despite the fear of failure. Personal courage is certainly not something that comes easily to most of us. It takes emotional and psychological strength to face our fears and insecurities, stand up for our beliefs, and take responsibility for our mistakes. But it is this type of courage that allows us to become the best versions of ourselves, to live fulfilling lives, and to reach our full potential.

Picture this: you're standing on the edge of a cliff, looking down at the water below. You know you want to jump, but the fear of the unknown is holding you back. It's the same feeling you had when you first learned to ride a bike or drive a car. But in order to overcome that fear, you need that courage we're talking about. Personal courage is all about taking that first step, even when you're not sure what the outcome will be. And when you do take that first step, it's amazing what can happen. Suddenly, the world opens up to you, and you start to see things in a whole new way.

It's important to highlight that personal courage isn't just about the big things, like jumping off a cliff or starting a new job. It's also about the little things, like speaking up for yourself or trying something new. It's about accepting imperfections and moving forward by building tolerance to the inevitabilities of life. You can do all the techniques to be a better person, such as acting opposite to your instincts, understanding your thoughts, reframing them, and dealing with your inner critics and noise, but these are just the tools to make it easier for you to develop tolerance. And the first step towards making the best out of these tools will require that personal courage concealed somewhere within you. That willingness to take the first step is what will make the entire difference.

Remember the time you learned to ride a bicycle? It was the willingness and the idea of freedom of going around the neighborhood and seeing people walk on the pathway while you zoom your ride past them. It was this personal courage and willingness that made you take the first step despite knowing you might fall down. So maybe the next time you find yourself standing in a certain situation, remember: it's the first step that's the hardest. But with personal courage and an inclination to embrace the indefinite, you can take that step and discover a whole new world of possibilities.

Life is a journey that's full of surprises, both good

and bad. And while we can't always control the events that happen to us, we can control how we respond to them. That's where tolerance and personal courage come in. Tolerance is often thought of as simply being accepting of others, but it's much more than that. It's about recognizing the diversity and complexity of the world around us and being open to different perspectives and ways of being. It's about having the humility to acknowledge that we don't have all the answers and being willing to learn from others. On the other hand, personal courage is about having the strength and pliability to face the challenges that life throws our way and being willing to take risks.

Let me tell you, it is not something that can be taught or bought, but rather it is something that we must foster within ourselves through self-reflection, determination, and persistence. When we tap into our personal courage, we can become our own superheroes, capable of achieving things that we set our minds to. It's a power that resides within each and every one of us, waiting to be unleashed.

Like being a surfer, riding the waves of life, it's not about finding the perfect wave with no bumps or obstacles in sight, but rather about having the skill and bravery to navigate through the rough waters. Just like a surfer, personal courage is not about being daring but rather about being willing to confront your qualms and overcome them. It's about having the flexibility to get back on your board after each fall and the determination to keep paddling forward even when the waves are crashing down around you.

Every surfer knows that each wave is different and requires a different approach. Similarly, personal courage is about having the pluck to face the tests that are specific to you and your own unique circumstances.

It's about recognizing that every challenge is an opportunity for growth and learning and that sometimes we just have to ride out the storm.

You can say Personal courage is like a muscle that we all possess, waiting to be flexed. It doesn't require a grandiose act of bravery to be impactful. It's the small yet significant actions we take every day that tests our courage and help us grow. Perhaps it's standing up to a coworker who is belittling others or voicing our opinion in a group discussion, even when we know it might not be popular. It could be taking a leap of faith and trying something new, even when we feel scared or unsure.

In today's world, where uncertainty and change seem to be the norm, having personal courage is essential. It helps us face challenges head-on, rather than avoiding them out of fear, ultimately making us become more resilient and better equipped to navigate life's ups and downs. But the beauty of personal courage is that it's not a fixed quality. It's a skill that can be honed and strengthened over time. Every time we step outside of our comfort zone and face our fears, we become a little braver and a little more confident in our abilities.

In nature, have you ever seen a butterfly emerging from its cocoon? Just like a butterfly, courage requires time, patience, and perseverance to develop fully and come into its own. The caterpillar spends its early stages of life inside a cocoon, a protective shell that shields it from the outside world. In the same way, we all have fears and doubts that prevent us from taking risks and stepping outside of our comfort zone. But eventually, the caterpillar must break free from its cocoon to become the beautiful butterfly it was meant to be. This requires a great deal of effort and struggle, as the butterfly must push and fight against the confines of its cocoon.

Similarly, personal courage requires us to break free from our chains of dread and hesitation, push past the limitations we have set for ourselves, and take bold steps toward our goals and dreams. It may be difficult and uncomfortable at first, but just like the butterfly, the end result is a beautiful transformation that is truly worth the effort - freedom from afraid.

And as you would set out on your journey, just like the butterfly, you would realize that success is not just about achieving your goals, but also about the journey itself. It's about facing your fears and challenges with a combination of tolerance and courage, where tolerance will help you navigate through the rough patches, keeping you grounded and centered when the going gets tough and courage would enable you to take risks and push through your limitations. Both courage and tolerance will help you face your fears head-on and emerge stronger on the other side.

Always remember, whenever you overcome a challenge, you build your courage and reinforce your belief in yourself. As you do so, you may begin to contemplate the significance of tolerance. You might ask, *why is tolerance so important?* For one, being tolerant is an incredibly satisfying and personally rewarding experience. It allows for growth, understanding, and embracing the richness of diverse perspectives. When we have developed tolerance, we feel a sense of accomplishment and pride in ourselves. When we practice it, we become more engaged, and attentively focused on the task at hand. This heightened state of awareness can help us overcome fear and self-doubt, which are common barriers to acts of courage. Consequently, tolerance provides a sense of confidence and motivation, empowering individuals to take courageous actions.

Moreover, building tolerance can help you in developing skills and expertise in your personal action, which can also contribute to your ability to act courageously. When a person is skilled and knowledgeable in a particular area, he or she may feel more capable of handling challenges and taking risks, which are essential components of courage.

The balance between tolerance and courage is crucial. Tolerance without courage can lead to complacency, while courage without tolerance can lead to recklessness. Together, they provide a sense of freedom and confidence, empowering you to tackle challenges come your way.

Embracing Your Inner Brave

The human experience is rife with fear. It's a natural response to the unknown, the indeterminate, the unfamiliar, which is ultimately inevitable. This can be paralyzing, leaving us stuck in place, unable to move forward. And yet, the first step towards bravery is not to eliminate fear altogether but rather to acknowledge and accept its presence.

Suppressing or ignoring our fears only gives them more power, allowing them to grow and fester within us. It's like trying to hold a beach ball underwater - the more we push it down, the more forceful it becomes when it inevitably bounces back up. Instead, when we acknowledge and accept our fears, we take away their power. We realize that fear is a universal experience, something that every person on this planet has felt at one time or another. It's not a weakness but rather a natural response to the world around us.

And when we accept our fears, we can begin to move forward despite them. We can take that first step towards bravery, towards courage, towards the life that we truly want to live. We may not eliminate fear altogether, but we can learn to work with it to channel it into something positive and transformative, and that's developing tolerance!

As we draw to a close of this piece of writing, let us marvel at the awe-inspiring beauty and potency of courage where it all begins and from where we all begin our journeys to healing, recovery, and being better humans. This personal valor and grit are not only about confronting peril or venturing into the unknown but finding the audacity to be true to ourselves and confront life's challenges with boldness and receptivity.

Like a warm, glowing fire that burns within us, courage is a spark that can light the path ahead, illuminating our way through the darkness of uncertainty and doubt. And as we face life's tasks, the fire of valor can grow, spreading its warmth and light throughout our being. When we have the courage to be ourselves, we are tending to this inner flame. And as we tend to it, we develop tolerance, where the fire burns bright and robust, fueling us with energy and motivation.

So let us nurture the fire of courage within us, tending to it with care and attention. Let us feed it with our victories, no matter how small, and let it grow into a roaring blaze that can light up even the darkest of times. For with the fire of courage burning within us, we can face inevitabilities that comes our way, knowing that we have the strength and determination to overcome them!

Thank You!

Dear Reader,

As I sit down, penning down the last words of this book, I'm overwhelmed by the depth of emotion that fills my heart. You're holding in your hands not just a book but a piece of my heart that I've poured into these pages. Your decision to join me on this journey means the world to me.

Writing "Building Tolerance to Life's Inevitabilities" has been a ride of self-discovery and an endeavor to share insights that I believe can truly make a positive impact on your life's path. Life isn't always a walk in the park; it's full of ups and downs, twists and turns. But here you are, ready to tackle those bumpy bits with a smile. Thank you for being open to the idea that we can learn, grow, and become stronger through it all.

I hope you find some gems of wisdom and practical nuggets within these pages. My goal has been to share some ideas that might make those tough moments a bit easier to handle. Life's challenges don't define us; how we face them does, and your decision to explore this book is a pat on the back for your own courage. As you flip through, my hope is that you'll find little sparks of inspiration that help you turn those "oh no" moments into "I've got this" moments.

I want to thank you for giving me the chance to be a part of your journey. Remember, life's a team sport – we're all in this together, learning and growing as we go.

Here's to embracing life's curveballs and finding the silver lining. Thank you for being an amazing reader!

Warmly,
Dr. Trent L. Culver

Reference Notes

[1]   Heimpel, S. A., Wood, J. V., Marshall, M. A., & Brown, J. D. (2002). Do people with low self-esteem really want to feel better? Self-esteem differences in motivation to repair negative moods. *Journal of Personality and Social Psychology, 82*(1), 128.

[2]   Beck, Judith S. (1995). Cognitive behavior therapy: Basics and beyond. *The Guilford Publications.*

[3]   Larsson, A., Hooper, N., Osborne, L. A., Bennett, P., & McHugh, L. (2016). Using brief cognitive restructuring and cognitive defusion techniques to cope with negative thoughts. *Behavior Modification, 40*(3), 452-482.

[4]   Larsson, A., Hooper, N., Osborne, L. A., Bennett, P., & McHugh, L. (2016). Using brief cognitive restructuring and cognitive defusion techniques to cope with negative thoughts. *Behavior Modification, 40*(3), 452-482.

[5]   Watkins, E. R. (2008). Constructive and unconstructive repetitive thought. *Psychological bulletin, 134*(2), 163.

[6]   Moseley, J. B., O'Malley, K., Petersen, N. J., Menke, T. J., Brody, B. A., Kuykendall, D. H., & Wray, N. P. (2002). *New England Journal of Medicine. NEJM, 347*(2),

81-88.

[7]   Stinckens, N., Lietaer, G., & Leijssen, M. (2013). Working with the inner critic: Therapeutic approach. Person-Centered & Experiential Psychotherapies, Leuven University Library. *Publisher: Routledge.* 12(2), 141-156.

[8]   Kaplan, S. (1995). The restorative benefits of nature: Toward an integrative framework. *Journal of environmental psychology, 15*(3), 169-182.

[9]   Ulrich, R. S. (1983). Aesthetic and affective response to the natural environment. *Behavior and the natural environment, 85-125.*

[10]   Howell, A. J., & Passmore, H. A. (2012). The nature of happiness: Nature affiliation and mental well-being. In Mental well-being: International contributions to the study of positive mental health. *Dordrecht: Springer Netherlands. (p. 231-257).*

[11]   McMahan, E. A., & Estes, D. (2015). The effect of contact with natural environments on positive and negative affect: A meta-analysis. *The Journal of Positive Psychology,* 10(6), 507-519.

[12]   Russell, R., Guerry, A. D., Balvanera, P., Gould, R. K., Basurto, X., Chan, K. M., & Tam, J. (2013). Humans and nature: how knowing and experiencing nature affect

well-being. *Annual review of environment and resources, 38,* 473-502.

13   MacKerron, G., & Mourato, S. (2013). Happiness is greater in natural environments. *Global environmental change, 23*(5), 992-1000.

14   Levordashka, A., & Utz, S. (2016). Ambient awareness: From random noise to digital closeness in online social networks. *Computers in human behavior, 60,* 147-154.

15   Kwee, M. G. (2012). Relational Buddhism: Wedding KJ Gergen's relational being and Buddhism to create harmony in-between-selves. *Psychological Studies, 57*(2), 203-210.

16   Soler, J., Pascual, J. C., Tiana, T., Cebrià, A., Barrachina, J., Campins, M. J., & Pérez, V. (2009). Dialectical behavior therapy skills training compared to standard group therapy in borderline personality disorder: a 3-month randomized controlled clinical trial. *Behavior research and therapy, 47*(5), 353-358.

17   McQuillan, A., Nicastro, R., Guenot, F., Girard, M., Lissner, C., & Ferrero, F. (2005). Intensive Dialectical Behavior Therapy for Outpatients with Borderline Personality Disorder Who Are in Crisis. *Psychiatric*

services, 56(2), 193-197.

[18]   Bryant, F.B. (2003). Savoring Beliefs Inventory (SBI): A scale for measuring beliefs about savoring. *Journal of mental health, 12*(2), 175-196.

[19]   Fredrickson, B. L. (2004). The broaden–and–build theory of positive emotions. Philosophical transactions of the royal society of London. Series B: Biological Sciences. *The Royal Society Publishing. 359*(1449), 1367-1377.

[20]   Tugade, M. M., & Fredrickson, B. L. (2007). Regulation of positive emotions: Emotion regulation strategies that promote resilience. *Journal of happiness studies, 8*(3), 311-333.

[21]   Schueller, S. M. (2010). Preferences for positive psychology exercises. *The Journal of Positive Psychology, 5*(3), 192-203.

[22]   Lyubomirsky, S., Sousa, L., & Dickerhoof, R. (2006). The costs and benefits of writing, talking and thinking about life's triumphs and defeats. *Journal of Personality and Social Psychology, 90*(4), 692.

[23]   Bryant, F. (2003). Savoring Beliefs Inventory (SBI): A scale for measuring beliefs about savoring. *Journal of mental health, 12*(2), 175-196.

[24]   Schueller, S. M. (2010). Preferences for positive

psychology exercises. *The Journal of Positive Psychology, 5*(3), 192-203.

25   Hill, P. L., Sin, N. L., Turiano, N. A., Burrow, A. L., & Almeida, D. M. (2018). Sense of purpose moderates the associations between daily stressors and daily well-being. *Annals of Behavioral Medicine, 52*(8), 724-729.

26   Hill, P. L., Turiano, N. A., Mroczek, D. K., & Burrow, A. L. (2016). The value of a purposeful life: Sense of purpose predicts greater income and net worth. *Journal of Research in Personality, 65*, 38-42.

27   Burrow, A. L., & Rainone, N. (2017). How many likes did I get? Purpose moderate's links between positive social media feedback and self-esteem. *Journal of Experimental Social Psychology, 69*, 232-236.

28   Davis, C. G., Nolen-Hoeksema, S., & Larson, J. (1998). Making sense of loss and benefiting from the experience: two construals of meaning. *Journal of personality and social psychology, 75*(2), 561.

29   Isaacowitz, D. M. (2005). The gaze of the optimist. Personality and social psychology bulletin, 31(3), 407-415. *Sage Journals.* Doi.org/10.1177/0146167204271599.

30   Seligman, M. E. (2006). Learned optimism: How to change your mind and your life. *Vintage.*

31   Boyer, W., Jerry, P., Rempel, G. R., & Sanders, J. (2021). Explanatory Styles of Counsellors in Training. *International Journal for the Advancement of Counselling, 43*, 227-242.

32   Conversano, C., Rotondo, A., Lensi, E., Della Vista, O., Arpone, F., & Reda, M. A. (2010). Optimism and its impact on mental and physical well-being. *Clinical practice and epidemiology in mental health: CP & EMH, 6*, 25.

33   Steptoe, A., Wright, C., Kunz-Ebrecht, S. R., & Iliffe, S. (2006). Dispositional optimism and health behavior in community-dwelling older people: Associations with healthy ageing. *British Journal of health psychology, 11*(1), 71-84.

34   Chang, E. C., & Sanna, L. J. (2001). Optimism, pessimism, and positive and negative affectivity in middle-aged adults: a test of a cognitive-affective model of psychological adjustment. *Psychology and aging, 16*(3), 524.

35   Hirsch, J. K., & Conner, K. R. (2006). Dispositional and explanatory style optimism as potential moderators of the relationship between hopelessness and suicidal ideation. *Suicide and Life-Threatening Behavior, 36*(6),

661-669.

[36]   Martínez-Correa, A., Reyes del Paso, G. A., García-León, A., & González-Jareño, M. I. (2006). Relationship between dispositional optimism/pessimism and stress coping strategies. *Psicothema, 18*(1), 66-72.

[37]   Segerstrom, S. C., Taylor, S. E., Kemeny, M. E., & Fahey, J. L. (1998). Optimism is associated with mood, coping, and immune change in response to stress. *Journal of Personality and Social Psychology, 74*(6), 1646.

[38]   Tindle, H. A., Chang, Y. F., Kuller, L. H., Manson, J. E., Robinson, J. G., Rosal, M. C., & Matthews, K. A. (2009). Optimism, cynical hostility, and incident coronary heart disease and mortality in the Women's Health Initiative. *Circulation,* 120(8), 656-662. Doi: 10.1161/CIRCULATIONAHA.108.827642.

[39]   Rasmussen, H. N., Scheier, M. F., & Greenhouse, J. B. (2009). Optimism and physical health: A meta-analytic review. *Annals of behavioral medicine, 37*(3), 239-256.

[40]   Scheier, M. F., Matthews, K. A., Owens, J. F., Magovern, G. J., Lefebvre, R. C., Abbott, R. A., & Carver, C. S. (1989). Dispositional optimism and recovery from coronary artery bypass surgery: the beneficial effects on physical and psychological well-being. *Journal of*

Personality and Social Psychology, 57(6), 1024.

41   McNulty, J. K., & Karney, B. R. (2002). Expectancy confirmation in appraisals of marital interactions. *Personality and Social Psychology Bulletin, 28(6),* 764-775.

42   Lench, H. C., Levine, L. J., Dang, V., Kaiser, K. A., Carpenter, Z. K., Carlson, S. J., & Winckler, B. (2021). Optimistic expectations have benefits for effort and emotion with little cost. *Emotion, 21*(6), 1213.

43   Fredrickson, B. L. (2001). The role of positive emotions in positive psychology: The broaden-and-build theory of positive emotions. *American psychologist*, 56(3), 218.